UNVANQUISHED SPIRIT

Surviving Life's Challenges
Through Faith

E. V. WEAVER

"for though the righteous fall seven times, they rise again,
but the wicked stumble when calamity strikes."
Proverbs 24:16 NIV

Disclaimer
The events and conversations in this book have been set down to the best of the author's ability, although some names and details have been changed to protect the privacy of individuals.

THANK YOU

Heavenly Father, thank you for always being by my side, for hearing my prayers and answering them. For knowing my needs, bringing me peace and for Your guidance.

To the most loving and thoughtful man I know, my husband. You are my best friend, and my rock, thank you for always being there. To my three beautiful children, you are God given. Thank you for all the love and joy you bring me.

Mrs Miggins, my oldest friend, thank you for your encouragement and support in writing this book and for always answering my phone calls when I had doubts and questions.

Thank you also to my small team of friends who acted as proof-readers and editors, your help has been invaluable. I could not have done this without you. Thank you again for journeying with me.

I want to acknowledge and thank Paul Manwaring and Neil Thompson for letting me use their inspiring quotes. Thank you for sharing your testimonies and all you do.

A QUICK NOTE FROM THE AUTHOR

This first book is many things. First, it is an account of the many events and situations I have been through in my life, my memoirs. It also acts as a cathartic experience for me. It is a reminder of who I am today and more importantly everything God has brought me through, stronger and more grateful to Him than ever before.

The conversations and comments between the characters in this book are actual conversations that took place. Some of the descriptions in a few of the chapters are limited because these are all I can remember. The important thing to focus on here is the incident happening at that moment.

I apologise to the reader in advance, as you may be left wondering, what happened next? If you find yourself asking this question, it is because even I do not know and it is too painful for me, even to this day, to try and find out.

I wrote this book eleven years ago, but I was too angry and hurt at the time to write the final chapter. After more than a decade, I feel the time is right to share my story and to encourage you to seek God in every dark and joyous event in your life. I believe He is always there with us even though we may not know it or feel Him at the time. I want to tell you to never lose hope or give up, and if you haven't started yet, I urge you to embark upon the incredible journey with Him, as soon as possible.

As the book progresses, I hope you will slowly recognise God working in my life, as He walks with me over the years, especially as He becomes even more tangible in my next book, 'Victorious Spirit'. The names of the characters have been changed to protect their identities, along with names of places.

CONTENTS

INTRODUCTION

One of the many questions people ask when you first meet tends to be, "where do you come from?" and "what do you do for a living?" But, when you're a Christian, one of the questions is, "when did you become a Christian?" So many people can remember the exact time and place when they experienced God for the first time. The person asking the question is intrigued to hear which of the many amazing ways you became a Christian. When was that moment in time when your life changed forever? Did you have a 'Road to Damascus' experience? Did you see Jesus standing in your room? Or did you go to bed one night having prayed and woken up the next morning to a life redeemed and healed? These are just some of the ways people experience it.

But it is only in the last several years, as I have become truly engaged with my new Christian family, that I have been asked this question. I have to say, I feel a bit annoyed when asked, or maybe it is more my reply that makes me feel incensed along with a feeling of, how dare people ask me this question? And how I shouldn't have to answer it in the first place. Much to my disappointment when comparing myself to others, (the one thing we should never do!) I did not experience any flashes of light. Nor did I hear God's voice speaking to me in the middle of the night although I did years later. My answer has always been, very matter of fact, "I've always been a Christian for as long as I can remember."

My experience of coming to know God has been a long and gradual one. It took many years before I truly recognised and acknowledged His faithful presence in my life. It was in that moment of realisation, I decided to reciprocate and wanted to be a part of - what was up until now - a one-sided relationship with Him, all coming from His side. From that moment on, my life began to change for the better.

Some people consider themselves Christians simply because their parents were. Unfortunately, that doesn't make them a Christian, not in the true sense of the word, or because they were Christened when they were a baby, and there's a Christening or Baptism certificate somewhere in an old, battered suitcase in the loft to prove it.

I think the question we should be asking each other is, "Do you know who God is?" "Are you aware of everything He can do for you?" "Do you have a relationship with him?" If you do, "What is that relationship like?" Because, if we are completely honest with ourselves, if we truly understand who He is, and what He stands for, everyone would want to have Him in their life and recognise Him for who He truly is. It is that simple.

I digress. As I say, my relationship with God has been a very slow and gradual one, strengthened over more than thirty years. It has been a long journey. It's like any friendship when you first meet, you ask questions about each other, you slowly get to know more about each other and then the more you begin to know them, the more you learn to trust them - and that takes time. Sometimes you just click, and other times it can take weeks, even months, and then after years of spending time together you know they will always be there for you, regardless of what time of day or night it is. A relationship with God is exactly the same, but so much more and sometimes it is hard to comprehend.

It's not until I look back do I see His hand in so many scary, sad and painful situations in my life, as well as the joyful ones. I wrote this book eleven years ago. It was written with the eyes of a hurt child, in pain, with anger and some disbelief. On rereading it for the first time in eleven years, parts of it have had to be rewritten from the perspective of where I am now. Because now I am redeemed, the wife of a church pastor and a prayer leader in my home church. I also help coordinate a national prayer line in my local area, responding to people calling from across the whole of the UK and beyond, people who are desperate for prayer. I'm a different person to who I was when I first started writing this book.

I can't believe how far I have come. Like I say, it's been a long journey. God has brought me to this point for a reason; just as you are reading this for a reason. He had a plan amidst everything I have been through, and I know He was with me throughout, even though I couldn't feel him at the time. There was always something there, in the room, deep inside of me, telling me I wasn't alone and to keep pushing forward.

Before you start reading this book, I would like to kindly ask you to do so with open eyes and a compassionate heart. Some parts of this book may seem to glamorise things, but that was never my intention. I'm just telling you what happened the only way I know how, with the only memories I have of that moment. I've tried to rewrite things so many times, but the words always stay the same. I can't write about something I didn't feel at the time; I can't describe something I didn't see; I can only say how I felt, at the time, in that moment.

Paul Manwaring, member of the senior leadership team at Bethel Church, Redding in the USA, summed my life up brilliantly; "He wastes nothing, He gets you ready" and He has! He uses everything for good, no matter how painful it was. Neil Thompson, one of the directors and leaders from ESST, (Edinburgh School of Supernatural Transformation in the UK) put it this way, "With the redemptive power of God, the worst events become the brightest future". And they do!

If you look back with God's love in your heart, hopefully you will see He was with you. At some point in your life, an opportunity will present itself, for you to use and draw from your experience of hurt and pain, to help others who are going through similar circumstances as you have. And when you're ready, God will draw people to you, people only you can help with whatever it is that they're going through because you will understand their pain. You will be the one to empathise with them, have the understanding and then be able to share your love and encouragement.

Before I can tell you where I am now and where I'm going, I first need to tell you where I've been.

"He wastes nothing, He gets you ready."

Paul Manwaring

Member of Senior Leadership Team,
Bethel Church in Redding, California, USA

Chapter 1

Sunday Lunch, England February 2003

I sought the Lord, and he answered me; he delivered me from all my fears. - Psalm 34:4 NIV

Sunday morning, I awoke feeling snug and cosy. I revelled in the warmth under the duvet, created by Liam's and my body during the night. I shuffled over and hugged him as he slept peacefully, the best way to start your day on a cold winter morning. Before children, we never got out of bed without having had a morning cuddle, a peaceful moment to ourselves before each of us heading off in different directions to work but since their arrival, these moments had become increasingly rare. The saying "nothing will ever come between us" has a whole new meaning once you have children. They are always in the way, especially in the middle of a lovely warm, king-size, Mummy and Daddy bed. By the time they have woken you up and jumped all over you, the last peaceful moments of Mummy and Daddy time are out the window. You find yourself downstairs in your dressing gown, with a packet of Rice Krispies in one hand and a bottle of milk in the other, serving breakfast to two, hungry, growing boys dancing around you with their demands of the day. Your day has begun. There was a relaxed feel about the day ahead, with the promise of a lazy lie-in for the first time in a long time with nowhere to rush off to. The only thing we had planned was Sunday lunch at Terry and Amanda's. Terry always cooked a lovely lunch. Roast lamb was on the menu with all the trimmings served with a selection of French wines, that, mixed with great company, was the perfect recipe for a relaxing Sunday afternoon. The day could only get better. Liam sometimes worked late but thankfully, not last night. It made a change for me not to have to walk around the house on tiptoes, trying to keep the noise down so he could get as much sleep as possible. Had he been working, it would be 5.30 in the morning before he came to bed, so I would try to let him sleep till at least eleven-thirty. Had it been me going to bed at that time, I wouldn't emerge until at least one o'clock in the afternoon. Liam didn't mind only having a few hours' sleep as this meant we could spend more quality time together as a family and enjoy our day. This ideal Sunday morning scenario was a rare event, the weight of the Sunday newspapers on the bed, a cup of tea on the bedside table and the television at the end of the bed showing some children's programme. The children as they sat on my feet, mesmerised while I tried to snuggle under my duvet and attempt to get five more minutes. An attempt that always failed miserably, typically I would end up sitting up and watching the children's programme along with James and Oscar, their excited little faces turning towards me giving me a running commentary.

After having mustered the energy to drag myself out of bed to get the boys and myself ready for our lunch date, I thought I should phone my mum who lived in Spain to let her know where I was going to be that day, so if she needed me, she knew to call my mobile. I had called her earlier in the morning while I was making the tea to check how she was feeling but forgot to tell her we were spending the rest of the day at Amanda's.

When she answered the phone, I instantly knew things were not right. I could hear her trying to catch her breath over the phone. She was struggling to breathe and couldn't say a word. All I could hear was the noise coming from her chest, a rattling, wheezing noise. My mother used to describe it as a "roo-roo" noise. I tried to stay as calm as I could so not to panic her even more, but inside me, alarm bells were ringing. I asked if she was alone; it was clear she was. "Mum, it's okay, put the phone down, I am going to call the bar downstairs and get them to call an ambulance for you."

Frantically I rummaged for the phone number of the bar to tell them what was going on. There was no one else I could call who could get to her immediately. They would have to call an ambulance for her. I couldn't call from England. I had to act fast, it was an emergency. The owner, Paco, had gone to the cash and carry, but Sebastian, the bartender, and Eva, the cook were there. They were in the middle of redecorating. I explained what was happening to mum in her apartment upstairs and asked them to call an ambulance immediately, then run upstairs to be with her. I put the phone down, slightly more at ease knowing someone would be with her now and the ambulance was on its way. At that moment, I knew I had to be with her. I had to catch the first flight out to Barcelona. There was a flight leaving from Luton in the next hour and a half with one of the low budget airlines. I had to make that flight; if I did, I could be at the hospital by six o'clock. Thankfully, Luton airport was only twenty minutes away from my house.

After calling the bar, I rang Nuria, my mum's cousin who for the past two weeks had been taking care of her. As it happened, she had gone back to her own house for a couple of days rest over the weekend. I told her what was happening and to get to mum's house as soon as possible.

She later told me she arrived just as they were putting my mum into the ambulance and was able to accompany her, so she wasn't alone.

I tried to call Pedro and Mercedes who were close friends of mum, and who had agreed to keep an eye on her and be there if she needed anything, but only the cleaning lady was in to answer my call. She gave me Mercedes' mobile number, but there was no answer.

I grabbed my passport and handbag, that was all I needed. I was on my way. I called Enrique, the waiter who had worked for us for a few years. His wife answered, explaining he was out in the park with their little boy and to try his mobile. I didn't have time now after having tried to contact everyone else.

As soon as the plane touched down, I called Nuria to get an update and to check how mum was doing. I had been in the air for one hour and forty-five minutes without being able to do anything, just praying everything was going to be alright. I had no way of knowing what was going on. "Dear God, please let me see my mum again. Please don't let her die, but if she is going to die, don't let her go before I get there." I wanted to be with her and make sure she was as comfortable as possible. Nuria assured me that for the moment mum was stable and doing well and Enrique was on his way to the airport to pick me up and bring me straight to the hospital. I couldn't understand how Enrique knew I was on route. I hadn't left a message with his wife because I didn't want to worry him. As it turned out, when he returned from the park, he phoned my house and with his limited English managed to make himself understood, and Liam had told him I was on my way. Liam had told him my time of arrival, which was around 5.45 p.m. As I left the arrivals lounge, I found him waiting for me. It was so good to see a friendly face.

When I arrived at the hospital, mum was extremely uncomfortable and not feeling too good. She was suffering with pain in her back, and the bed she was in was hard and lumpy which was making matters worse. She was wearing an oxygen mask and hooked up to a drip. She looked exhausted and although pleased to see me all she wanted to do was go home. A nurse entered the room to check her oxygen, which still hadn't reached the satisfactory levels. The nurse told us mum needed more rest and she should stay in hospital for at least a few more hours, but mum was refusing to stay any longer, she couldn't bear the pain in her back and the uncomfortable bed.

Whenever a nurse or doctor entered the room, she would smile and say to them, "Look, this is my daughter, I call her and say I am ill, and she jumps on a plane and comes flying from England. She has to leave her husband alone with her two sons to look after me and look, here she is." Brimming with love and pride. Sometimes I would get annoyed with her when she introduced me to people saying, "Look at my daughter, isn't she beautiful? Just like her mother. She's my baby."

It was so embarrassing. I was no longer a baby or a little girl and hadn't been for quite some time. I was a married woman with two children of my own and not long turned thirty.

I left the room to speak to the doctor and ask if they could keep my mum in hospital permanently since she had been so ill and clearly struggling to breathe. "I am sorry, but we cannot admit your mother as we don't have any of her medical records. We have done everything we can for her. If I were you, I would phone the doctor who is treating her and ask him to have her admitted to the correct hospital, where she will get the appropriate care and attention." I couldn't believe what I was hearing. They couldn't turf her out of the hospital as she was, she wasn't well enough. What if it happened again? This was the second time I had jumped on a plane to be with her. The last time was just two weeks ago, but she seemed much better then. I had only agreed to leave her because Nuria was staying with her as a live-in home help. Mum had insisted I return to England to be with Liam and the children. I was in a difficult situation, it wasn't practical to bring the boys with me, and to have two young boys running around the apartment would make mum feel worse. I had visited the local schools to enquire about registering them, with the view of us coming over to stay and care for her; at least they would be out of the way during the day. I had talked to mum about letting me stay in one of the three apartments she owned. My friend Chloe was willing to come over from England to be with the children and look after them whilst I stayed with mum in her apartment during the day looking after her.

The apartments were just across the road from each other, so during the night if mum needed anything, all she had to do was pick up the phone, and I would be there in minutes. I thought of every possible scenario of how I could be with her, but she wouldn't have it. "Pedro and Mercedes will come and visit me if I need them, you don't have to worry." It was true; at least they lived just a few streets away. We agreed Nuria would move in to look after her. At least they had the same character, were of the same age, and they did have a laugh together. It would do her good if she did stay. Nuria didn't have anything else better to do, she was retired, and would be getting paid, so everyone was a winner.

Mum was still in a lot of pain and extremely uncomfortable, she insisted on going home. She had a very forceful character when she wanted, one you didn't want to deal with if she was in a bad mood, or angry. I was unable to argue with her, especially in her state, and although her breathing was still not great, it had improved, so reluctantly I took her home.

By the time we arrived back at the flat, it was eight o'clock at night.

Mum went and lay down on the sofa where she had spent the last two months watching television and going through her extensive DVD collection. I covered her up with a blanket, it felt good to be back home, surrounded by recognisable things and home comforts. Straightaway I made mum a long-awaited cup of tea, and then went on to prepare her some chicken noodle soup with an egg in it, which we both loved. I then rang the bar downstairs to order a couple of cheeseburgers for collection ten minutes later. While waiting for the burgers I loaded the dishwasher and cleared the kitchen which was in a bit of mess -coffee cups piling up in the kitchen sink - and the worktop needed wiping down as bits of sugar and coffee granules had started to accumulate where mum had come into the kitchen to make a coffee and then headed straight back to her spot on the sofa before she became tired and breathless again. I cleared the newspapers from the floor, a makeshift litter tray for mum's two small Jack Russells, I assumed judging by the mess on the newspapers, hadn't been out for a walk in a couple of days. When you don't have a garden, old newspaper is the next best thing. It also prevented mum having to get up and down to let the dogs out on to the terrace. We did have an incredibly large terrace this was the reason why mum bought the apartment in the first place. It was like an oasis in the middle of the city. She was so lucky; it was something we always dreamed of and wished for. I let the dogs out for half an hour to get some fresh air, having been closed in all that time whilst I tidied up.

I kept a close eye on mum. I would have preferred her to have stayed in hospital, where I felt secure knowing there were people around who knew what to do should she have problems with her breathing again or if she stopped breathing altogether. I felt scared. I was worried about my mum and me. What would I do in that situation? I prayed she would be alright. I wouldn't have known what to do if mum suddenly died while we were alone in the flat. I knew there would be an ending soon, but when and how? I was so scared of being on my own with her. I was all she had. She was my mum for goodness sake; I couldn't abandon her. I wanted someone to come and take this all away from me and make it all good. I wished someone would be there with me, I didn't want to be alone.

Mum complained about her back pain, so I sat next to her, gently rubbing her back and praying for healing, anything to make her feel better. I just wanted her to feel better.

She was much happier and relaxed now having returned home. We lay snuggled up on the sofa together as we used to when I was little. She on her side with her knees bent, and I sitting snug behind her legs, obviously much bigger than years gone by when I was able to rest my head on her hips. There was a calmness in the air as we quietly watched the television, then she turned to me and said: "Evie, tomorrow at nine in the morning, you have to remind me to call my *gestor*. It is very important I call the *gestor*." (The *gestor* in Spain acts like a solicitor who draws up important documents ready for signing.)

"Yes, Mum," I replied. I knew what she was referring to and why, but I didn't want to let on. I wasn't interested. My only concern was getting my mum the correct care to make her feel better and more comfortable. We carried on watching the TV.

Mum's breathing wasn't particularly good, she made a lot of noise when she breathed, but it was the pain in her back that bothered her the most. As I gently rubbed her back, she relaxed, and it did soothe her for a short while. It was the coughing which started to unsettle her. It was a dry, irritable cough, the one that irritates the chest and the throat, but until you can reach it and cough it up, it won't stop. It was very bothersome, but if she could cough in the right way, then she would cough the phlegm up which was suffocating her and blocking the bronchioles of the one working lung. Her other lung had collapsed a few weeks earlier.

We turned the television off with the hope of getting some sleep. We both lay on the sofa for a couple of hours without success. Mum liked sleeping on the sofa, she did so regularly. She preferred it to her own bed; it was more comfortable. I think it was because she felt lonely in such a large apartment, her bedroom was right at the end of the long hallway and it seemed quiet and cut off from the rest of the apartment. It was a beautiful apartment with four good-sized bedrooms all facing the street, with plenty of natural light. In many Spanish apartments, the bedrooms are internal and natural light is minimal. If external, the view out of the windows is usually the bedroom of your next-door neighbour. Everything about this apartment was brilliant. The living and dining room were much larger than average, and as the apartment was a corner plot, the sun would shine in through the two large windows most of the day. In the summer we used to sit out on the large L-shaped balcony which looked out onto the park and gardens in front, we would swivel the television round and watch films in the open air whilst having dinner. Being outside at night was the only time you could comfortably stand the summer heat.

There were two bathrooms, one of which was part of mum's en-suite. There was a sizeable bath where she loved watching the boys splashing about and making a mess. She didn't mind as it was me who would clear up after. She loved it when the boys and I came to visit, that was when she was happiest. The flat itself was designed to a high standard throughout, with beautiful, polished mahogany furniture from a large department store. Mum did all her shopping there. She had come a long way to be able to shop in a high-end quality department store like that one.

After a while, we went to my bedroom where there was a large reclining armchair. I wondered if it would be more comfortable for her. We stayed there for an hour and a half with no relief to the pain, so we then went to her room to see if she would have better luck in her own bed. I lay next to her on the double bed. By this point, she was sad and fed up, unable to rest from the constant spluttering of coughs. I continued to massage her gently to try and alleviate the pain, but I too was tired. I hugged her like a mother hugs her child when she is sick. There was silence in the flat. Mum turned to me again, "Do not forget, tomorrow at nine o'clock I have to call my *gestor*, it is very important I call him." She had her serious look on her face, the look telling you to do as you are told, or else. As she said it, I could feel her starting to get agitated. She was desperate to make the call.

"Yes, Mum, don't you worry about it now. We'll call him in the morning." I didn't care about the call. I wasn't interested. I just needed her to remain calm. I believed in miracles; I still do. The oncologist told us she was getting better, and the tumours had reduced. Never give up hope; never lose faith.

She turned and looked at me, now with a repentant look on her face. "Evie, I have done a terrible thing. I don't want to tell you what it is, but I must speak with my *gestor* tomorrow." She wouldn't rest.

"Will you please stop talking and just relax." I started to cry.

"Don't cry, my darling. I know why you are crying." She took my face in her hands and said the same thing she had always said to me while I was growing up. "You know I love you more than anything in this world, and you are the best thing that has ever happened in my life. I have done lots of bad things to you, and I only wish that you forgive me. Evie, you know I have always loved you, don't you?" It was just her and I, alone again, like we used to be many years ago. It seemed we had come full circle. Tears were streaming down my face now. My mum was dying, and I couldn't do anything to make her better, to make it alright again. I wanted to go back to where we were before this nightmare started. Little did I know this was just the beginning.

"Yes, Mum, don't you worry about anything. There isn't anything I need to forgive you for. All that matters now is that you get better."

"Evie, will you please pray for me?" The room was spinning before me. No....! No...! No! I don't need to pray. You're not going anywhere. It felt like the last prayer before you die. Was she wanting the Last Rites prayed over her? She knew what she was doing. There was no vicar or minister here. I couldn't refuse to pray for her. I did as she asked, we prayed together, alone in her bedroom. It was three o'clock in the morning. I prayed to God for healing. I asked him to surround her with his love and presence, for him to give her strength and courage so she wouldn't be afraid of anything.

Mum insisted I go to bed and try to get some sleep. It had been a long day. I lay in my bed, exhausted unable to sleep, surrounded by the same furniture I had when I was in my late teens. It had taken till then for me to have a designed bedroom with matching furniture that mum was finally able to afford and had always wanted to buy for me. The cupboard, dressing and bedside table were all white with black edging. It was trendy back then.

It was already 5.30 in the morning, and I could hear mum in the other room. Every ten minutes she would start coughing again, trying to reach that part of the cough deep in her chest, doing her best to clear the airways or the irritation without success.

I kept my ears open, listening out to see if she needed anything, ready to go running to her in the other room. Finally, we managed to fall asleep for about two hours until 7.30 a.m. Daylight told us the night was over and we may as well get up. We both made our way to the sofa where mum lay down to watch the morning news and take her cocktail of tablets as part of her morning routine.

Monday

Her breathing was slightly worse this morning, but still she carried on as usual. With a couple of espresso coffees, we settled down to watch the morning news on the television. I filled up the big glass that lived on the table with fresh water, so that she could take her cocktail of medications and made sure she had a roll of tissues to hand. I gathered up some courage to try and get my mum to see sense. "Mum, listen to me. If you call your doctor and tell him how you feel, he will have you admitted to hospital where they will look after you and give you some magic medicine to help with the pain. They will have all your records and know what's best to do for you." By magic medicine, I meant morphine. She was in an awful state and needed some sort of help.

"They gave me some morphine last year, and it didn't do anything."

"That was because they only gave you a tiny bit. This time they will give you a higher dose until the pain goes away."

"We are in Spain, Evie, it is not like in England, they will not admit you into hospital just like that you know." She was starting to get annoyed, so I decided to leave it, not to get her worked up and aggravate her breathing even more.

"Okay then, but if your breathing continues the way it is, I am calling for an ambulance." I was starting to get nervous now as her breathing was getting worse. I was scared it would get to a point where we needed an ambulance immediately.

"No, you won't. I am fine," she asserted. The more I tried to convince her otherwise, the more worked up she became.

Nine o'clock came, and my mother was starting to get frantic because she couldn't find the telephone number for the *gestor*, so she made me call directory enquiries to find it. I gave her the number I had been given and she began to make the vital call she had been so anxious to make all night. I headed to the bedrooms to make the beds and to leave her to it. I already knew what this was about, but at that moment in time I didn't care. I just wanted to get my mum into a hospital. I heard her shouting from the living room, "Don't you tell me he's in a meeting, you always tell me the same thing. I want to talk to him. I want to talk to him right now!" Now she was angry. I ran down the hallway.

"*Mama*, please calm down," I whispered to her.

"Now you listen to me! I am very ill. I need to talk to him urgently, do you hear me?" She was screaming down the phone at the poor receptionist at the other end. I thought mum was going to have a heart attack as she was getting very flustered, which wasn't good at all.

The receptionist told her she would get the *gestor* to call her back as soon as he was free, and with that mum hung up the phone. She was incredibly nervous and uneasy.

Whilst mum was in hospital the first-time round, Doctor Gustavo, the pulmonologist, made an appointment for her to visit the pain management clinic, for pain relief for her back. There they had arranged for a nurse to come to the house twice a day and administer pain relief injections. If this didn't work, then mum was to call the clinic today, Monday morning, and let them know in order to get a stronger injection which should ease the pain for a whole month. Mum had waited all weekend to make the call to see if anything else could be done as now the pain was becoming unbearable. She called and explained how bad the weekend had been and the week running up to it. When the receptionist heard how bad mum sounded, she told her to hang up the phone, and said she would call her back in a minute. She was going to call Doctor Gustavo to check on some things. What she meant was my mum was dying and she needed to be admitted into a hospital right now. I already knew this by the way she was breathing. Very soon after, there was a call from Doctor Gustavo. Mum answered, but she was so tired and having trouble breathing, she passed the telephone over to me so I could make a note of the time and directions for an emergency consultation.

"I have made an appointment for your mum for this evening at 7.45 with Doctor Lopez. He will give her some morphine. She's in a bad way and could do with some morphine to help her rest. She already has an appointment for Wednesday to do a clearing of the lungs which I will do tomorrow at two in the All Saints Clinic. Okay?" He was very charming and helpful.

"Yes, thank you so much, Doctor Gustavo." All we had to do now was keep calm, relax and get plenty of rest. Tomorrow we could go to mum's appointment where the doctor would stick a tube down her throat to vacuum out the phlegm that was preventing her from breathing. Then she would be fine. He had already performed this procedure on her a couple of times before where he inserted a special stent-type thing to keep the bronchioles open, keeping the airways free and preventing them from collapsing. Mum was satisfied with the new arrangements, but I was now very uneasy because her breathing was not improving, on the contrary. It didn't feel right.

"Right, Mum, I'm calling for an ambulance to take you to hospital."

"No, don't. I'm fine." This only made her angrier.

Then, ten minutes later, the *gestor's* son called. I listened to how she agreed to an appointment being made for the gestor to come to our apartment on Wednesday evening at 7.30. In my head I was telling her to make the appointment for today as I didn't think she was going to be here on Wednesday, and this was all going to end up going pear-shaped.

I was suffering for my mother, for what she was trying to do and knowing it wasn't going to be carried out. She was desperately trying to right the wrongs she had done before it was too late. She put the phone down and stood up to go to the toilet. She was having difficulty breathing and walking. I put my arm around her waist to support her. Once safely back on the sofa, I picked up the phone and called the doctor back. "I am sorry to trouble you, but my mother is really ill, and she won't go to emergencies. Is it possible to have her admitted to a hospital where she can be looked after properly and get some oxygen and morphine?" I was extremely worried because she wouldn't let me help her and she was in a bad way.

"Look, Evie, if you want, I can admit her into the All Saints Clinic because it is clear she is very sick. I will call Doctor Lopez and get him to come and see your mum this afternoon and I will do the cleaning tomorrow morning." That was all I wanted to hear. They were going to take care of her.

"Thank you. I'm happy with that but could you please explain it to my mother for me? I would appreciate it." I turned towards mum and handed her the phone. "Mum, listen, it's Dr Gustavo, and he says he will admit you into the All Saints Clinic and there they will take care of you just like a queen. He wants to talk to you." I passed her the phone and let the doctor explain it all to her. She would listen to him and finally do as she was told. At last, my mother agreed and was resigned to go to hospital.

Without a moment to lose, I phoned for a taxi and grabbed some things we might need. I was desperate to get to the clinic, but it was on the other side of the city and the way things were going, we may well end up back in the Emergency Department, in the hospital in Cullera.

Cullera was just a ten-minute drive straight down the road along the dual carriageway. A couple of minutes had passed, and the phone rang again. It was Señor Jimenez, the *gestor* himself, the person who always dealt with mum's affairs. Mum, who was sitting on the sofa exhausted at this point, answered.

"What's the matter, Señora Santiago? You called the office earlier?" He was very cool, calm and collected, typical Spanish "mañana, mañana" attitude, nothing like what was going on in our house.

The tone in my mum's voice changed to relief and calm, thank goodness. She was very grateful to finally get hold of him. "Yes, I need to draw up some paperwork, I am very ill, and I need to talk to you. It's urgent!"

"What sort of paperwork do you need drawing up?"

"I need to change my will."

"Okay then, give me all the details and I will have them drawn up for you." Mum began to dictate everything she wanted doing.

"At the moment I have left everything to Pedro Francisco Rodriguez, and I want to change it all back to how it was originally. Everything in my daughter's name except one flat, the one in Calle Pamplona, No. 7." He asked mum to spell my surname, which she did with difficulty but began to get flustered with not being able to breathe well, she passed me the telephone.

"Hello, good morning, Evie, isn't it?" came the voice of the *gestor*.

"Yes, it's me." I felt awkward. I didn't want to be having this conversation. Now was not the time; we could wait a couple of days.

"Your mother wants to change her will and as you may have already heard, before she had left it all to Señor Pedro Francisco Rodriguez, and now she has made you universal heir except for one of the flats in Calle Pamplona, No. 7."

"Yes, very well." In my head, I was urging him to hurry up and get on with it. We had to go! Suddenly the doorbell went. What now? I couldn't believe what was going on. I asked him to hold on one minute while I answered the door. I rushed to the door and found the neighbour from upstairs, Maribel. She owned one of the shops at the entrance to the building where she sold home accessories and beautiful gift items. I left her on the doorstep to make her own way in and rushed back to mum. Maribel took one look at mum and didn't say a word, her mouth fell open, shocked at everything going on. I had to get back to Sr. Jimenez at the end of the phone to finish spelling out my surname. Finally, he ended by saying, "Right, everything is all done. All I need now is a copy of your passport and the old will and I will come to your flat on Wednesday as arranged. Okay?"

"Yes."

"Very well. *Adios*." And after all that he hung up the phone. I had a bad feeling I wouldn't be seeing him on Wednesday after all.

Maribel had to go downstairs as her husband was waiting for her in the shop. She just popped in to see how things were with mum after seeing her be taken away in an ambulance the day before. Now she had her answer. Not good!

By this point, the taxi had arrived and was waiting downstairs. I managed to get mum from the sofa to the dining chair, where I made her sit to try and catch her breath. I kept saying to myself, as long as I can get her to the clinic, she'll be fine. I just had to get her there before she got any worse. Maribel asked if I needed any help with anything. I asked her to wait for me downstairs and help me get mum into the taxi. We managed to reach the lift, but by now she was getting worse. We struggled to walk out into the street and had to stop every two paces for her to catch her breath.

Now we were at the point I hoped we would never get to. I had to think quickly. What was the quickest way of getting to the Accident and Emergency Department? In the taxi, which was already here and waiting? Or, should I call for an ambulance? In the time it would take an ambulance to reach us we could be already at the hospital.

We climbed into the taxi. Maribel helped support mum by one arm and me the other. "Please, take us to the Emergency Department in Cullera. Hurry, as fast as you can!" I told the taxi driver.

"No, no! They are waiting for me in All Saints!" Where she got her strength from, I do not know but even then, she started to get annoyed with me. She could hardly breathe. I wanted to tell her to shut up for once and do as she was told. I still couldn't, for fear of upsetting her.

She was adamant we had to go to the All Saints hospital on the other side of the city. We agreed to go up the road and try. I told the taxi driver to see what the traffic was like. As soon as I saw the traffic in front of us, I ordered him to carry on going round the roundabout and head straight for Cullera. Mum should have been in hospital ages ago. Her breathing was worse, yet she still managed to complain. "They are waiting for me," she struggled.

"*Mama*, for the first time in your life, will you shut up and do what I say! If we don't get to Cullera, you are not going to arrive at All Saints." I had my arms around her shoulders. She no longer had the strength to argue. That was the first time I had contradicted her; it was for her own good. Had she been feeling better she would have told me where to go speaking to her like that. The poor driver was so scared, one of his best clients was dying in his taxi.

"*Si, si,* let's go there as quickly as possible," the taxi driver agreed with me. He was beeping his horn and flashing his lights all the way down the road, going as fast as he could.

Mum's breathing was now minimal. As I embraced her in my arms, I kept encouraging her and talking to her. "You're doing great, Mum, hang in there, we are nearly there. Once we get there it will all be okay. It's going to be alright Mum. Relax and breathe nice and slowly. I'm here, Mum. We are very nearly there." She could no longer respond or do anything; she wasn't breathing.

We arrived at Cullera Hospital. I jumped out of the taxi shouting, "Oxygen, please, we need oxygen!" Some nurses came out in no real hurry, but as soon as they saw mum lying there in the taxi, they soon realised they had an emergency on their hands, and immediately a man lifted mum up in his arms and put her on a stretcher with some oxygen attached. They then wheeled her off inside, leaving me behind at reception to fill in forms.

Eventually, I found the room where they were treating her, but I was told to stay outside while the doctors and nurses did their thing. All was quiet inside the room while people were rushing in and out. What was going on? I felt as if I was starring in an episode of *ER* or *Casualty*. It was surreal. I was standing in the middle of a large hallway, full of lots of different people coming and going. They were going about their business, visiting people who may have just twisted their ankle or cut a finger. My mum was in a room, dying. She may be dead for all I knew. Couldn't they see what was going on? Something big was happening here, and they were carrying on as if nothing. I wanted to scream at them, but I felt they wouldn't hear me and wouldn't be interested anyway. I looked to see if there were any TV cameras anywhere. This sort of thing didn't happen to my family or me. Shortly after I heard mum shouting. "I can't breathe!" Her voice was full of panic and fear. One of the doctors came out to see me to get some of her backstory, so I explained to him what had happened, where we were supposed to be heading and why. I asked if he could phone the other hospital and tell them we were here. After a while, I was allowed to go into the room and see her. She was wearing an oxygen mask, and they had hooked her up to a drip and a bag. I sat down beside her and held her hand. She just lay there, looking at me. She was frightened. The doctors left us alone. I listened to her breathing and scared each breath was going to be her last. I prayed to God, if He was going to take her that He do so while she was sleeping, without suffering or pain and with me by her side.

As I lived in England and she in Spain, she always complained how one day she would die alone in her flat with the dogs, and no one would realise she had died until it was too late.

Dying alone was her biggest fear. I could only pray I would be with her, and she wouldn't die alone. Shortly after, a nurse told me Doctor Lopez was working in this hospital and was currently searching for a bed for mum to be admitted right here. I felt a huge weight lift from my shoulders. It was such a relief; I knew they were going to look after her. I went back into the room where she was resting. "Mum, you'll never guess what? Doctor Lopez, the doctor who you were supposed to see tonight, he is right here in the building, he knows you are here, and he is looking for a bed for you in the other main hospital up the road. So, you don't have to worry about a thing. He'll be over to see you later, but first, you must rest." Already mum was starting to feel a little bit better. Surprisingly enough, this time round in hospital, her back wasn't hurting as much as it had done the previous day. She was relieved with the news I had just given her.

At around four or five o'clock, Mum's bed was ready and waiting for her in the other hospital which was a ten-minute drive away. We had to wait for a specially equipped ambulance, one carrying oxygen to take her. Two hours we waited before it arrived. It had been a busy day for the ambulance service, we didn't mind the wait.

Eventually a young, attractive porter came into the room to help mum gather up all her things and ready to go. Mum had perked up a fair bit by this point and was now flirting. She was impressed with how nice and attentive he was.

He lifted her up and out of the bed placing her gently on the stretcher, then strapped her in making sure she wouldn't fall off. Then he covered her up with a blanket, protecting her from the cold night air. It was now dark outside, and mum had been in a nice warm room all afternoon, he didn't want her to catch a chill. "Oh, isn't he a nice young man? Isn't he handsome? Do you have a girlfriend?" The young man blushed but went with the flow. Mum was laughing with him. It was nice to see, I laughed with them knowing how embarrassing mum could be, but in a nice way.

Once at the other hospital, we entered the lift and went up to the nineth floor. When we came out of the lift, it was as if we were in a lovely four-star hotel. The corridor was tastefully decorated and lovely paintings hung on the walls. She had been allocated a private room with a television and an ensuite bathroom. The room was painted in a warm pastel green colour and was welcoming and comfortable. It looked nicer than some hotel rooms I had stayed in. It was lovely and not at all like a hospital. Mum herself was pleasantly surprised and seemed happy, calm and well attended to. Every half hour, a cheery nurse would come in to check on her. "How are you feeling? Are you alright? Do you need anything? Are you in any pain?" They were all lovely and caring. My mother was amazed, she finally let herself relax. By the time we had arrived on the ward, the doctor we were supposed to see had already finished for the day but would return first thing the next morning. We were okay with that.

Mum was in a comfortable state, and the nurses had given her some medicine to help dissolve the mucus, so she could breathe more easily. The nurses arranged for dinner to be brought to the room which mum chose from the menu. She didn't eat very much. She lay in her bed watching television, and I sat next to her holding her hand. We were exhausted. We tried to sleep but only managed short naps. The noise from mum's breathing was loud and unsettling, I couldn't relax. I watched her as she slept, observing every detail, every little wrinkle.

How had we ended up here? I felt as if I were in a film. This was all a dream; I would wake up soon and everything would be back to how it was before. Yes, the arguments, the crying, the emotional blackmail, the fallouts. But, at the end of the day, this was my mum, and I loved her. No matter what anyone said or how badly she may have treated me, I was here for her, and I wasn't going to leave her for a second. I watched and listened to her every breath. With each breath, the gaps became longer and longer. I sat anxiously wondering if that was her last one and if she had died. How did it happen? Dying?

How would she react? How would I react? I had never seen someone die before. All these questions ran through my head. I wanted to be prepared, I wanted to be strong for my mum, and not run out of the room in a panic which is what I wanted to do. I was afraid. How selfish was I? How the heck was my mum feeling? I couldn't leave her to face this alone. I didn't want to face this alone either. Apart from mum's breathing, the floor on which we were on was very still. The night went by without a lot of sleep but not as bad as the previous one.

Tuesday

The sun shone through the window with a beautiful view of Barcelona as far as the port.

That was the good thing about being on the nineth floor, the view. Not that mum was able to appreciate it, so I described it to her instead. The new shift of nurses came in and introduced themselves to us and did all the usual checks, blood pressure, temperature, oxygen levels. A lady came up from the restaurant and asked us what we would like for breakfast. She took our order, coffee, and a *magdalena*, (which is a Spanish fairy cake people usually have with their morning coffee), that, or a doughnut. She said she would be back shortly. I switched on the television, so we could watch the morning news and see what the weather was going to be like. Probably another sunny day in Barcelona, even if it was a little on the cold side.

I remained in the same place I had been all night, holding mum's hand throughout and sleeping with my head resting on the side of the bed. My back was starting to hurt now as I wasn't sat in the most comfortable of positions. I had been crying sporadically through the night while mum slept, and now I was drained. I just rested my head again by mum's side and promptly fell asleep, happy knowing she was awake, alert, and comfortably watching television. About an hour later, I awoke to find mum sitting up in bed as I had left her, just looking down at me. The TV was still on, but the volume was on mute. I looked over to the table at the end of the room and saw her breakfast sitting there on a tray, her coffee stone-cold and untouched. "Mum, your breakfast is cold, why didn't you wake me up to pass it to you?"

"You were sleeping like a baby. I didn't want to wake you up. You needed to get some rest." She had been watching me while I slept, just as she did when I was a child.

"Oh, Mum, you must be hungry." I got up and went to order her some fresh coffee. She couldn't function in the morning without her double espressos. Today, however, she was doing very well. She was peaceful and relaxed.

We would exchange glances as if to say we both knew what was happening here, but it was all going to be alright. I had always been with her when she needed me most, and I was here now. Some visitors turned up which pleased her, the cleaner from work and one of the neighbours. While they sat with mum, I dashed back home as quickly as I could to sort out the dogs and to check they had enough food and water, and that they hadn't made too much of a mess. I went and changed into some clean clothes and had a good wash, grabbed some bits for mum and returned to the hospital as quickly as possible. By the time I arrived back, to my surprise, mum was tucking into a bowl of soup, followed by some chicken and chips, then a yoghurt. She ate it all and thoroughly enjoyed it. We hadn't eaten a proper meal for a couple of days, so she must have been starving. She was laughing with her visitors telling them about the porter and how nice all the nurses and doctors were. I hadn't seen her this relaxed in a long time. It was like she didn't have any worries anymore. They had all been taken care of for her. She would glance over to me and smile, a warm smile, which didn't need any words.

Shortly after the visitors had gone, the doctor who was on his rounds came in and checked mum over. He looked over her records and had a little chat, asking her about her pain levels and how she was feeling. He was a tall man in his long doctor's white coat. Mum enjoyed speaking to him and answered all his questions. When he had finished, I followed him out of the room, and I stood very still as he talked to me in the corridor. He was saying things which I didn't understand, and I couldn't hear him very well.

I am fluent in Spanish as I went to school there and have spent many years living there on and off, but he must have been speaking a different type of Spanish to the one I knew. "You need to realise your mother doesn't have long to live. She is riddled with cancer. She has cancer all over her body." Right, I could cope with this, but it was weird, because the other doctor said she was actually getting better! How can she be riddled with it? I thought he must be talking about another patient, possibly the one in the next room. Right, I get that she doesn't have long to live, initially I was told she only had until Christmas if she was lucky, but then another doctor said she was doing well. It was now February. She can rest a bit and then I can take her home, and she can rest even more there.

I thought I had better check. I took a deep breath and asked the dreaded question.

"How long exactly?"

"We are talking hours." Oh, for a moment there I thought he said "hours". Then he went on to say, "I cannot believe how this woman is still standing and so strong, she shouldn't be here seeing how ill she is. I am amazed. If you want to phone anyone, you need to do it now."

What the heck was he talking about? She is fine, look at her, she is sitting up watching television, chatting with all the staff. She was alright now; she had had some oxygen. I had asked Pedro ages ago if he could speak to his medical contacts, to see if we could get some small oxygen tanks for home, for when she needed it, like some patients have. I knew that's what they did in England. Why was this down to me? Why was I an only child? Where was my mum's husband? He should be dealing with this, not me. Oh yes, I remember now, my parents were divorced, and my dad had just died four months ago. Right, I suppose I had better get on and deal with this then.

I thought I had better phone Pedro and let him know what this idiot doctor had said. He would sort it out. He was my mum's best friend and always knew what to do. He was like a son to her. I phoned Pedro straightaway while I was still in the corridor. Mum trusted him, and so did I. I hadn't seen him in a long time, so I explained to him what the doctor had told me and for some reason he started getting angry with me. He didn't believe me and demanded to speak to the doctor himself. I was confused as I didn't consider him as immediate family, but as it was him what harm could it do? I found his attitude somewhat surprising, considering that, at the end of the day, I was the one here alone with my mother, who, according to the doctor, could pass away at any moment. Liam was back in England. I wanted to share my pain with someone, and Pedro was giving me attitude over the phone when I least needed it. I asked the doctor to speak to Pedro to confirm what he had just told me, and then I hung up. Immediately I called Liam and my uncle, my mum's brother to tell them what was happening. As soon as Liam put the phone down, he started looking for a flight, praying he would get here in time.

When I reentered the room, mum was fast asleep. They had given her a small sedative so she could rest, and some morphine for the pain and an injection so she could breathe more easily. She looked so relaxed. Finally, she was getting some long-awaited rest, and her breathing had much improved. It was around 1.30 in the afternoon when she fell asleep, not long after finishing her lunch.

She had been fast asleep for a few hours without moving or making any sound, apart from the slight rattling noise as she breathed. I sat beside her, and all was still. While still asleep, mum called out to someone, "Robert?" her voice sounded pleasantly surprised to see Robert. I couldn't see him, but mum gave the impression she definitely could, and he was there in the room.

At that moment, I began to cry. Was my dad really in the room? Had he come for my mum? Was he waiting for her? I was excited, confused, and unsure all at the same time. Part of me believed he was there with us and the other part of me told me mum must be dreaming. I preferred to believe my first thought.

When my uncle and his family arrived in the evening, she awoke for a few minutes. I wondered how she could wake up just as they arrived and not before. Mum chatted very briefly and then they left her to fall straight back to sleep again. Not long after my uncle had left, Pedro came with his friend, Ramon. I was stunned to see Ramon, as I hadn't seen him in nearly eight years. The last time I saw him was when he came to mum's business for a couple of free drinks as he was in the area; she hadn't spoken about him for ages, he was more of an acquaintance than a friend. Ramon himself was around mid to late fifties but looked much older because of partying so hard.

Pedro and Ramon just strolled into the room, making a bit more noise than you would expect in a place where someone was dying. Pedro didn't even acknowledge me. They stood by the side of the bed, trying to wake mum up by prodding her and pulling at her fingers. I felt disgusted and didn't understand what his problem was or why he was acting in such a way. He was so cold towards me. I hadn't done anything to him or his family, we always seemed to get on well enough. I was starting to get annoyed but thought I was in the wrong place to show it. "Leave her alone, let her sleep, she hasn't slept well in days, and she can't breathe very well when she is awake."

"No, she will be alright, she's strong. She will be home by Saturday. I will send a taxi to pick her up tomorrow and take her home." Whose home he was talking about, I wasn't sure. I was horrified by what he was saying. I was standing right there, and they were talking as if I were invisible. Soon they departed and it was just the two of us alone again. I spent the night holding her hand and singing all her favourite songs to her.

As the sun rose in the morning, the horizon seemed to be made up of all the colours of the rainbow. I thought this must be a special, magical moment when a new day is dawning, which you could only see if you were looking in the right place, at the right time. It felt like a secret, as if this is where heaven was. The door to heaven was opening and waiting for mum to enter. It felt like an event that only happened every so many years or centuries, and I felt privileged to witness it. As mum slept, I told her what I was seeing and how beautiful it was. I was waiting for something to happen, but I sensed a peace whilst waiting. I knew I wasn't really on my own. I saw a plane not too far away making its descent, preparing to land at Barcelona airport. The airport was only five minutes away and I knew my husband was on that plane. As she slept, I kept talking to her, I knew she was listening to every word I said.

"Mum, you have a special visitor coming to see you this morning. Your favourite son-in-law is coming to see you." She used to say he was the best son-in-law in the world and how much she loved him. Today was Wednesday, and my mum was still with me. I kept checking to make sure she wasn't too hot, and if so, I would uncover her, if she was too cold, I would cover her up again. Mum's cleaning lady, Laura, turned up along with Enrique's mum, Isabel, and Nuria, mum's cousin. They arrived all at the same time. We all stood around the bed, talking quietly amongst ourselves hoping she might wake up. She had not moved or woken since my uncle had left. Then suddenly, my husband's voice entered the room before he did, showing off the very little bit of Spanish he knew.

"Hola! Buenos Dias."

As Liam entered the room, Laura said in a surprised voice, "Look, Evie, look at your mum, your mother's eyes just moved for the first time when she heard her son in law." We all looked at her intently. "Look, look at how she knows he's here. Look how happy she is," said Laura and Nuria.

Liam went and sat on the bed next to mum and talked to her for a little while as she slept. He couldn't stay long; he had come straight from the airport. Enrique picked him up and was downstairs with my two boys in the car. Enrique couldn't speak English and the boys couldn't speak Spanish, so it seemed unfair to leave the boys for too long in a car with someone they didn't really know. He said goodbye to mum, and I told her I would be back in a second. I had to go and say hello to the boys as they hadn't seen me since Sunday. I was reluctant to leave her for too long. What if she died now, just as I was downstairs? How would I feel about that? I gave the boys a quick hug and explained how Yaya, Spanish for grandmother, wasn't very well, and I had to go and be with her. They wanted to come with me, but it was impossible and out of the question. I gave Liam the keys to the flat so he and the boys could go back to the apartment. They would be happy there. They had lots of their toys and videos there to keep them amused until I could join them.

When I got back to the room, mum's breathing had changed. She seemed emotional that her son in law had visited her.

40

The nurses confirmed what was happening, so I sat on the side of the bed, facing her with my arms either side of her. I kept talking to her all the time, talking to her softly and gently. Reassuring her everything was going to be alright, and I was right here with her. Mum's cousin was standing by the side of the bed crying, "No! No! No!"

Suddenly, mum opened her eyes wide and looked straight at me. It was her and I.

"It's okay, Mum, it's okay. There is nothing to fear. Dad's waiting for you. I'm here, Mummy, I love you. It's all going to be okay now." She just looked at me peacefully, listened, closed her eyes and she was gone.

****

Looking back there was a peace and reassurance that was almost tangible. How many times had my prayers been answered without me even realising it at the time? Even my thoughts of fear and anxiety were calmed at every step. Yes, I was anxious and worried, and I had no control over the situation I was in; but I could control my reaction. My reaction was to pray, pray with all my heart without knowing if anyone was listening, but I prayed none the less. It was all I could do.

Chapter 2

The Early Years

The light shines in the darkness,
and the darkness has not overcome it. - John 1:5 NIV

My earliest memory is extremely blurred. I can only remember the smallest detail, and yet it means so much and is so precious to me that I deliberately hold on to it even more. I have it hidden in one of my many memory banks, safely locked away. I like to know it's there should I wish to take it out and replay it occasionally and wonder how different my life would have been, how different all our lives would have been and which direction our paths would have run.

I am walking in a large room in a hospital. The size of the place impresses me, and I am holding someone's hand. It is the hand of someone very tall and strong. I can see beds either side of me and we are walking towards a lady in a blue dressing gown at the end of the room. She is holding a baby, a new-born baby. I cannot see the baby's face; I only remember the large room and the blue of the lady's dressing gown. It would be July, two months away from my second birthday.

A few years later, once I had learnt to read, I read a small newspaper cutting which lives in a small, silver picture frame, placed at the bottom of a photo. The photo is of a woman with thick dark brown hair, a seventies-style haircut, cradling a new-born baby. She looks proud and happy, posing for the photo to record this moment of happiness forever. She wears a beautiful blue dressing gown. My mum looked beautiful and young in the photograph. The newspaper cutting reads; *Mrs Santiago, of Pembroke Road, woke up last Saturday morning to find her eight-week-old baby boy dead in his cot.*

My eight-week-old brother, Jeremy, died of sudden infant death syndrome. My mum once told me she went to feed him at around six in the morning, but as he was sleeping so peacefully, she didn't want to disturb him, so she let him continue enjoying his sleep. When she went back to him two hours later, he was no longer with us.

I can't begin to imagine the grief and sorrow my parents must have gone through. The existence of my brother was never discussed nor the events that transpired, or who came forward to support them during that harrowing period in their lives. I don't know whether any counselling was available, let alone offered. All I have is the photo of the brother I never knew.

I believe this was the starting point when my parents' marriage began to shatter into pieces.

They divorced when I was two. I suppose I could say this is where my journey and travelling commenced. I'm not talking vast distances here, only from south London to the centre of London to begin with. During the week I stayed with my mum, and at weekends my dad would come and pick me up in his black London taxi and take me to stay with him. After my parents separated and divorced, my dad did what a lot of men do in the same situation and moved back in with his mum and her second husband. I loved spending my weekends with them.

My nan's house was big. It had four floors, including a basement. I lost count of the number of bedrooms on the top floors as I rarely went up there, I didn't need to as all the rooms were rented out.

By the time dad and I arrived on a Friday night, nan had already left the house, dressed up in all her glad rags and sparkling jewellery and was at the local social club playing bingo. I knew she would be waiting for me with a big kiss and a great big hug. Those nights were special. It was a different type of life to the one I lived with mum. My dad would find somewhere to park his taxi and then try to calm me down before walking into the club as I would be bursting with excitement. "Right, Nanny is playing bingo now so when we go in, we have to be quiet and go sit in the bar area and wait for her to come out once she's finished. Okay?"

"Okay, Daddy."

You could already hear the hustle and excitement of people having fun and letting their hair down on a Friday night as you walked through the doors. It was so exciting for a young girl of my age. I would have been around four or five. As the doors opened, I could see the lights from the bar twinkling off the glasses that hung upside down above the bar area. Colours shining from the selection of bottles on display at the back of the bar, in front of the mirror, the light reflecting and beaming through them. Grown-ups were coming and going, to and from the bar. Their hands full, carrying pints of bitter and lagers, the gin and tonics, port and lemons. Packets of dry roasted nuts and the picture of a pretty lady at the back of where the packets were displayed, wearing a pretty swimming costume with a big smile on her face.

I was allowed copious amounts of lemonade and a couple of packets of crisps - I was a slightly tubby little girl when I was young. My nan would come out at half time when all the ladies came to get their refills. I would spend my time running around the bar area playing with some other children whom I had never met before. Once the bingo session was over, my nan would come and join my dad and her second husband. At some point in the evening, everyone would turn and focus on the door with some excitement, it was the shrimp man. The shrimp man came in dressed in white, carrying a wicker basket full of various types of seafood. He had a basket full of goodies – cockles, shrimps, mussels, whelks – and we always had some. I loved the shrimp served in a polystyrene cup with a little wooden fork. My dad enjoyed the whelks, but I found them a bit too chewy for my liking. It was all sold by the pint glass. I could never understand how you could eat a pint of shrimp.

One night, however, things did not turn out to be as much fun as they usually did. As I sat in the corner with my drink, I could see there was a bit of a commotion going on over by the bar. A group of people were gathering around my dad, trying to hold him down. They were trying to stop him doing something, I didn't know what or why. He had grabbed hold of an empty bottle and was aiming to crack it over my nan's husband's head. There was a lot of screaming and shouting going on, and I could see my nan was upset, pleading with my dad to stop what he was doing. My dad and her husband had been arguing and my dad was very upset.

This was an extreme occasion as my dad would never hurt a fly. Never in his life did he ever lay a finger on me or even tell me off. I could run rings around my dad and get away with so many things, and I knew it. My dad disapproved of my nan's husband, I don't know why, but I didn't like him much either.

I'm not sure if it was the same night or not, but on this occasion, we were back at my nan and dad's house, and I was with my dad in his bedroom. There was lots of shouting going up and down the stairs. My dad opened the door to his bedroom and was standing on the landing yelling at my nan and her husband. Dad wanted to chase after him down the stairs, but my nan stood in his way, trying to stop and reason with him but to no avail. There was such a lot of struggling going on and thuds from pushing and shoving. My nan was crying.

I sat in the corner of my dad's bedroom crouching on the floor with my hands up to my ears and my eyes tightly shut. My dad slammed the door and locked it behind him, my nan and her husband decided to leave him to it and went downstairs. Nan was very upset. He hadn't meant to slap her as she had got in the way of him trying to hit her husband. I know he would never have intentionally hurt her. My nan was worried for me on my own with my dad feeling the way he did, and I was scared myself, but only because of what had just happened, yet; I knew I was safe with him. He made me up a bed out of some cushions from a sofa in the room, and I lay there quietly.

I never had my own room when I stayed at my dad's. My bed was always on the sofa in the living room. I spent many years sleeping on the sofa as I grew up. I loved it, as I didn't know any different.

My nan would tuck me in, leaving the living room curtains slightly open. Directly outside the house was a streetlight which gently lit the living room. Nan explained how the light would watch over me during the night as I slept and keep me safe. I was never scared, and always promptly fell asleep.

In the morning, I would wake up bright and early and sit crossed legged on the floor in front of the television, watching my favourite programme, *Sesame Street*, while nan prepared some cornflakes with warm milk. I'd sit there eating my flakes enthralled until the programme finished.

I was never bored as two doors down from nan's house lived my dad's brother and his wife, with their two boys. They were slightly older than me and I spent a lot of time with them at their house or across the road where there was a playground. Sometimes my aunt would take me shopping with them and other times my dad would take us all to the park to play and run amok. It made a change playing with all their boy toys. Their bedroom floor was covered with green plastic soldiers, carefully positioned for battle and we would play for ages. The boys had two puppets from The Muppet Show. One was Fozzie Bear, and the other one was Kermit the Frog. We found some material and tied it over two chairs to form a makeshift theatre, and we would put on shows and perform with the puppets. My cousin Harry did a great impersonation of Fozzie Bear, and I nearly wet myself laughing. They were so funny, and I loved spending time with them. Growing up, I always talked about them as if they were my brothers. I had such a great time.

Sometimes nan and I would go shopping. We used to get the bus from the top of the road and go to the market. I loved the market with all the different colours and smells, with strange men shouting at the top of their voices telling you to come and buy their produce. I remember one time when it was raining and starting to get dark, I was getting cold and tired. The glow from the lamps hanging above all the stalls gave off a warm glow, and a feeling that the stalls and the stall holders had been there for years. Fruit and vegetables wrapped in brown paper bags, which, if they became wet from the rain, they would fall out all over the place. My favourite bit was when my nan bought sticky buns to take home. I couldn't wait to get back to the house and sit by the fire and watch *The Six Million Dollar Man* while eating my sticky treat. We were always back in time for the football results. I'd sit on the floor against my nan's chair in front of the gas fire with its fake burning log effect. Nan's table lamp beside her gave the room a snug cosy warmth to it. It was a beautiful lamp with carved little naked cherubs all around with a simple shade to go with it. Nan would sit hunched over the coffee table with various bits of paper scattered all around. While the football results were announced, no one was allowed to say a word, move or even breathe.

Of course, I couldn't keep quiet all the time and as soon as I started to say something, a stern finger would go up in the air as a warning that if I carried on, there would be trouble ahead.

My nan always made me laugh. She was such a jolly happy soul. She loved a drop of whisky and always had a bottle down by the side of her chair. A bottle would last a whole week, sometimes two. It was her special little tipple. Her forte was making cakes. Saturday mornings were spent making rock cakes, fairy cakes, scones and then sausage rolls and egg and bacon pie. The point was to make enough to last throughout the week, but it rarely did. By the time dad and I discovered the freshly baked rock cakes and my cousins had popped in to say hello, they were gone by Tuesday. Thinking back, I remember how my nan seemed always to have a cigarette hanging out of her mouth. Sometimes she would even forget it was there, as the white paper would burn away and leave in its place one long line of ash. "Nan, you need to put your cigarette in the ashtray, it looks like it's about to fall."

"What? Oh, yes, thank you, Evie." She would be so engrossed with the job in hand she didn't realise that the cigarette was burning itself out. In the morning, she would walk around in her mauve dressing gown while she went about her chores. The main bathroom was on the floor downstairs in the basement. You had to pass it to get to the kitchen. I hated walking past it as it was always dark and silent. Every time I had to go to the kitchen, I would run with my eyes straight ahead and avoid peering down the stairs at all costs. Even as a teenager, I would have nightmares about the place. So bizarre. The basement downstairs was a self-contained apartment, which my nan rented out to a young gentleman. She was quite the entrepreneur.

All the spare rooms were let out to people I did not know and never saw. She told me of times when they hadn't paid the rent on time, so she would change all the locks and throw their belongings out on the pavement. No messing about with her, a strong independent woman. My real grandfather had died a few years before I was born, of a lung condition at the age of fifty-five.

Nan was such a happy person who loved going out dancing, singing, and playing bingo, it was a good thing she met someone new to go and have fun with. She remarried someone with whom I'm sure she had certain things in common with, otherwise, what would she have seen in him? However, I can't bring myself to say his name.

Chapter 3

Old Men

The LORD himself goes before you and will be with you; he will never leave you nor forsake you.
-Deuteronomy 31:8 NIV

It's interesting how our past experiences can affect us and determine how we react to life and each other, further down the line. But it is in the understanding of our past, by recognising who we are today, by refusing to believe the lies that may have shaped us and by acknowledging and embracing our true identity, that we can then move forward into our future in freedom.

Liam, I, and the children lived in Australia for a short period of time, six months to be exact, and whilst there I awoke one morning having an anxiety attack, because of a disturbing dream I had just had. For a couple of days previous, I had been concerned about an upcoming appointment someone had booked with me for that morning, and I was agitated about it. It's probably what triggered my dream. I would have been far happier cancelling the appointment, but I was determined to keep the 10.30 a.m. slot as it could be the start of my something big.

On top of everything else, I had the beginnings of a cold, which was getting worse, and I felt awful. A few years earlier I had graduated from college as a holistic therapist, and I was now self-employed and trying to build a customer base. My speciality being reflexology, aromatherapy, and body massage. It fitted in perfectly with the children and Liam. Being my own boss meant I could choose when and where I worked. Whilst the boys were at school and nursery, clients would come to my house for a treatment and in the evenings, I would go to them and give my clients a massage in the comfort of their own home. It was great, I had no overheads to worry about, and I enjoyed it. All my clients were women.

This was all new though, we were no longer in England, we were now living on the other side of the world. I had to start all over again.

Liam had been offered a job as the general manager for a chain of Texas-style steak restaurants. As soon as we arrived in the country, we busied ourselves trying to find somewhere to rent for the short term. We had put our house up for sale and, once it had sold, we intended to buy a place somewhere in Queensland and stay there permanently. Liam had two weeks to familiarise himself with his new surroundings and settle in before starting his new role. Prior to arriving in Australia, I had found us a lovely little holiday home to rent for the first week while we inspected all the local towns and villages within a set radius surrounding Liam's newfound job. We eventually settled for the up-and-coming, fast-developing town called North Lakes just north of Brisbane. It was going to be beautiful. It already was, but there were still more developments planned. It was clean and modern. I registered the boys in the new local school and Sophie in the local nursery where she could make lots of new friends. It was an exciting time.

Liam was working more hours and days than initially expected and everything was so much more expensive than we originally anticipated, so I set about looking for a part-time job.

One day, whilst I was out and about in the car over in the next town, I drove past a gym where I saw they were advertising for a massage therapist. I went inside to find out more and spoke to Tom, the manager. They were offering a free treatment room and they didn't want a share of the money, they just wanted to look good, offering their members extra services and benefits such as sports and body massage and reflexology: I was in luck. My English qualifications were valid in Australia, and with my experience, they said I could start whenever I wanted. The treatment room was shared between a number of therapists, each offering different treatments. Tuesdays and Wednesdays, the room was set aside just for me. I also offered mobile treatments where I would do home visits as well. After a couple of weeks of clients booking treatments at the gym, Tom asked if I was able to visit one of the club members at his home. He had kindly given my number to a man and told him to call me. The man had been a member at the gym for a few years now and was used to having regular massage treatments in the home of another therapist, who had a treatment room set up in her back garden. Recently, travelling to the therapist's house had become an inconvenience for him, mainly because of his age and his mobility. As I advertised as a mobile therapist, I was an interesting alternative to the man's usual massage therapist. I was excited someone required my services, but not so pleased when I heard it was for a seventy-year-old man. Something deep inside me started to stir, so much so that I was now lying in my bed having a panic attack.

I forced myself to get out of bed and get ready for my appointment. With anxiety still simmering inside of me, I managed to calm myself down and I pulled up outside the address given to me over the phone. I was still anxious and tried hard to control myself. I told myself that this could be something good, regular work and word of mouth travels fast. I hoped he would be happy with his treatment. Not everyone was like my nan's husband.

I went in and introduced myself. It was a beautiful house, nicely decorated and a pleasant, calm environment. I asked where he would like me to set up my couch, and he showed me to his living room where there was a big, fluffy tabby cat, sleeping on the sofa, completely relaxed. The man was genuinely nice and polite. "That's Charlie. I can move him out of here if you like?" the man said looking at his beloved cat.

"No, that's fine, he's no problem, he seems very content." I said, as I went over to Charlie the cat and started stroking him. He was soft and just lifted his head slowly towards me, with his eyes slightly open. "Hello, Charlie, who's a lovely boy then?" I stood up, still smiling at the cat, thankful he had calmed my nerves a tiny bit. "He's lovely," I added.

"Oh, my goodness," the man exclaimed in surprise. I felt a startling fear rise within me.

"What? What's the matter?" I asked, trying hard to contain my growing anxiety.

"Charlie, my cat…"

"What about him?" I couldn't handle any surprises. "What's wrong?"

"He never lets anyone touch him or go near him. With you, he didn't even flinch."

"Okay?" This guy was weird. Dear God, please help me stay calm.

"There is something about you. He hates people, and yet he let you stroke him." The man was freaking me out now.

"Right, well, why don't you tell me a bit about yourself and your medical history and what it is you need today."

The man told me of his arthritis, the aches and pains he had been suffering with recently and how he was going less and less to the gym.

All the while, I was fighting the anxiety inside me. I was trying to get a grip of it, but it was slowly creeping out of control. "Right, we'll take it gently then so not to aggravate any of your joints. If you would like to remove just your shirt and shorts and cover yourself with the blanket provided, then we'll begin." My heart was beating faster and faster. The man started to undo the buttons of his shirt as I left the room. I left him to get ready and once he was covered up, I would go back in. But I couldn't do it, I couldn't go through with it. "I am so sorry; I am going to have to leave. I am actually not feeling very well, and I don't want to pass it on to you. I am so, so sorry about this." I had to get out of there as soon as possible.

"And also, I am concerned about the pains in your muscles. I wouldn't want to make them worse."

"But that is exactly what I need to alleviate the pain. It'll be okay, honestly."

"No, I'm sorry, I think you would be better off with a physiotherapist. I am sorry."

"I am more than happy for you to do this because I know there is something about you. I can sense it." What was he talking about?

"I am so sorry." I collected my things as soon as I could and left. My past had come back to taunt me.

I understand where my hang-ups with older men come from; my nan's second husband. It's incredible how actions and words said or done years ago can stay hidden or unhidden for the rest of your life, and by doing so can change or alter the way you walk your path forever.

What I am writing here now has never been spoken about before. I am resurrecting my memories for the first time.

I remember when I was about four years old, maybe five, while spending the weekend with my dad and nan in Fulham. My dad had gone off to do something, so I stayed with my nan that day and accompanied her to help one of her friends move house. I recall her and her husband carrying boxes up and down lots of flights of stairs in a large mansion-type house somewhere in London. It had been divided into apartments. I was tired of going up and down the flights of stairs, so I was told to stay and wait at the bottom, and at the same time, I could keep an eye on the other boxes which were waiting to be taken up.

My nan must have decided she too was tired, as she remained upstairs in the apartment while her husband was left to do all the lifting and carting around.

Each time he came back down to collect another box, he would come over and kiss me on the lips. I wasn't sure what he was doing or why. It was like a "hello there" kiss and then he went on his way. I thought he was trying to be funny and playing some sort of silly game. I didn't know this game, it felt weird and bizarre, but he thought it was amusing. He would keep kissing me as if for a laugh. He kept checking no one was coming down the stairs and told me to be quiet and not to make any noise. My nan was not to find out about our funny little game. The more I told him how horrible it was and to stop it, the more he laughed and just continued. I felt confused at the time, but I trusted this person who had to be a good person because he was with my nan. Somewhere inside I knew it was wrong, but I didn't say anything just in case it was me who was wrong. I never said anything to my nan as I didn't want her to get upset with me or tell me off.

I remember the time when I was introduced to a particular make of camera. You only had to wait a few minutes for it to develop, it was part of the excitement. A photo emerged from the bottom half of the camera, grey at first, but then very slowly an image would evolve. You could buy a strip of cubes that you attached to the top of the camera, and they acted as the flash. I remember one day I was happily playing outside on my nan's doorstep. It was a lovely warm, sunny day when her husband came over to me. "Evie, Evie, come over here!" he beckoned to me excitedly.

"What? What is it?" I was very curious.

He was in a hurry to show me something. I was intrigued and a little excited. I thought he might have a present or some sweeties for me. "Come over here." He called me over to the stairs, which lead to the apartment on the lower level of the house, the basement or many years ago, the servant's entrance to the grand London houses. We went downstairs where no one could see us, hidden away where he could safely show me his secret. "Now, this is a secret. You mustn't tell anyone, okay?"

"Okay, what is it?"

He took something out of his pocket. He seemed quite proud of it and then turned it around so I could see his secret. I couldn't quite believe what I was looking at, let alone understand why this was being shown to me. With his camera, he had taken a photo of his penis to show me. I was shocked; it was the first time I had seen that part of the body and I was bewildered. I knew it was him because he had taken it with his dressing gown on; his chequered brown and green dressing gown with the rope-type belt. I recognised the gown straightaway. Why was he showing me this? I felt disgusted and confused. Somehow, I knew this was wrong. He then asked me if I wanted to see it in real life. He took it out before I could answer. I don't remember anything from then on.

Some mornings when I had woken up from having slept on my nan's sofa in the living room, I'd run into her bedroom and jump into bed with her and her husband while they laid there and did their crossword puzzles or read their books. My dad, in the meantime, would still be upstairs in his bedroom, fast asleep. He never woke up until much later. My nan used to be a crossword puzzle fanatic; she could sit and do them all day. At Christmas time she would be given crossword toilet paper as her present so she could do them while on the toilet. We all thought it was a highly amusing present.

It's not until now that I'm older, that I think back on the things that happened and question them. What really happened? If this is what I do recall, what are the things I don't? Were they my fault? Did I go looking for it? Did I flaunt myself? I was five years old or thereabouts at the time. Did I know what I was doing? I loved getting into bed with my nan for cuddles; she was an extraordinary person. She would tell me amazing stories about her life and the things she got up to when she was a little girl and how hard life was growing up during the war. I enjoyed snuggling beside her in bed with the light from her bedside table lamp lighting up her corner of the bedroom on a cold winter's morning while still dark outside. She always was an early bird. She would wake up around five in the morning, get up, make her first cup of tea and then bring it back to bed.

When she and her husband were ready for their second cup, she would get up and go along the hallway to the back of the house and make another brew. I stayed on her side of the bed to keep it warm for her return. He would then turn to me and say, "Oh, Evie, I have such a poorly tummy. Can you rub it better for me?" He would take my hand and place it on his stomach with his hand on top of mine. I did feel sorry for him, he had a stomach-ache so maybe I could help him and make it better. He would make my hand rub his stomach all around the lower part just below the waistline of his pyjamas. All the while, he would moan and groan and say how much better it felt. As soon as he thought he could hear my nan coming back with the tea, he would stop and push my hand away. Once he realised it was a false alarm, he retook my hand and continued showing me how to rub his stomach area just below the waistline.

After a couple of other incidences, I felt uncomfortable and knew I had to say something to my nan. I ran down the hallway to find my nan who had popped out to the kitchen during the adverts.

"Nan, Nan, he's being rude." I told her.

I don't know what I told her or what she asked, but sometime later, maybe a few weeks after, my nan told me she wasn't living with her husband anymore, and she was moving to Hertfordshire so she could be nearer to her daughter. She was leaving London, she was going back to the village where she was born and grew up, in the countryside near the farms and the rivers. It wasn't until years later that I learnt he had been going with other women, so she decided enough was enough. She left him and his drinking.

I never saw him again or liked to hear people talk about him. Even the sound of his name makes me cringe. It is because of this experience I can never look at older men without a suspicious eye.

Chapter 4

Latch Key Kid

*Start children off on the way they should go, and even when
they are old, they will not turn from it.*
-Proverbs 22:6 NIV

From the moment I started playschool, right through to primary school, my mum worked full time and I spent most of my time being looked after by different childminders. There are two main women whom I vaguely remember, and I had fun playing with their children. Strange how I had never wondered until now how much it might have cost my mum to send me to these ladies, where I stayed all day. I know childcare today is expensive, but I have no idea how much they would have charged back in the early seventies. They were friends of my mum's, but whether they were friends before she had chosen them to care for me or whether she befriended them while I was in their care, I have no idea. The vague memories I have are happy ones of playing, laughing, and growing up without a worry. It's funny the things one remembers, and the things we don't. Whilst at playschool, I remember playing with weird plastic, coloured shapes that slotted on to one another to create a tower and long pieces of straw-type sticks which clicked together to make shapes.

There are photos of me painting on an A-frame in a playground alongside Jane, daughter of one of the childminders, as she attended the same playschool. I am wearing a pink knitted kaftan-type cape thing so lovingly knitted by my nan, one of our many knitted Christmas presents. In the photo, I have a pudding bowl haircut, and

59

I am wearing a thick pair of pink national health glasses (they don't make them like that anymore) They should do though; they would last much longer. Yes, they made you look ugly but at least they were sturdy enough to last.

I remembered being taken back to Jane's house and being amazed by the tea we were given. Jam sandwiches and jelly. I thought this was amazing to be having jam sandwiches for dinner. They were cut into neat little squares, and it made a change from my home-cooked dinner which my mum lovingly prepared for me every night. I had a slight weight problem while I was growing up; I wasn't obese, but you could say I was a little on the chubby side.

It must have been tough for my mum in those days as Lucinda, the lady who used to look after me, didn't live just around the corner. When I was taken to Lucinda's house, my mum would wake up at 4.30 in the morning to get ready for work, then get me up a little while later and push me in my pushchair for a couple of miles through the back streets of south London and around the park in the freezing cold, not forgetting it would still be dark at that time of the morning. My mum walked everywhere because she couldn't drive, so wherever we went, we walked. Very occasionally did we catch a bus. I loved going on the buses but hated waiting for them. I would stand at the bus stop freezing cold, my feet like ice blocks, jumping from one foot to the other trying my hardest to keep them warm, but it was to no avail. Mum would wrap me up inside her coat and hug me tight to keep me nice and warm until the bus arrived. We huddled together like penguins. We were so close; I don't just mean in terms of proximity either. I loved being with my mum and spending time with her, I suppose this was because the time we did spend together was so rare.

After having dropped me off at the childminders, she still had another fifteen minute walk to where she worked in a coffee factory as a packer, where she had to clock in at six in the morning. It would generally take her half an hour in total to get to work.

During the summer holidays, I remember I was about seven years old going to visit my mum at work and having lunch with her at the staff canteen. My mum would go round introducing her little girl to everyone who worked there, whether they wanted to meet me or not. I must admit they were enchanted to make my acquaintance most of the time.

On Fridays I would walk from school all the way to the factory, which would generally take a good forty minutes. It was some distance for a little girl all on her own. I surprise myself thinking about it now, but then you just got on and did it and thought nothing of it.

I loved going to school, I loved every minute of it. I was now a big girl, in a big girl's uniform, attending a lovely school full of colour, music and singing. It was a Christian school, Church of England. We had assembly every Thursday morning when the local vicar from the church down the road would come and tell us incredible stories which I marvelled at and was intrigued by. One of the stories that struck me with amazement was about three men surrounded by fire and yet they didn't get burnt or hurt because God had protected them. They walked out of the fire completely unscathed. There was another man, his name was Daniel, some guards had thrown him into a lion's den overnight, but instead of any of the lions hurting or eating him, the lions just sat there. No harm came to him. We said prayers every Thursday, The Lord's Prayer and The Grace, which I repeated and knew off by heart, but never really knew what I was saying or understood. I joined the choir and loved singing at the various concerts we held. At Christmas time we were all given song sheets and Christmas carols to learn, which I rehearsed relentlessly every night in the privacy of my bedroom. We decorated parts of the school with big pictures and paintings of Bethlehem, and for some reason I felt something speak to me. I wanted to be in this village where people would sit on their roofs and admire all the funny little houses. I was fascinated; something had pricked my heart, in a good way.

Right from starting school, I used to wake up alone in the house, get myself dressed and have breakfast. My mum had already left for work at five in the morning and left me fast asleep in bed. Our friend and neighbour, Hannah, had a spare key and would come in every morning at around eight o'clock to wake me up and walk me to school. I was only five years old after all, so I couldn't very well walk to school on my own. I would do that when I was six. Hannah would say to my mum how good I was in the morning. Every time she came in, I was already sitting at the kitchen table tucking into my cornflakes, fully dressed and ready to go. Sometimes she would take me back to her house and I would sit and watch while the rest of her family went about their morning routine.

They had porridge for breakfast, something I hadn't had before and it didn't look very appealing to me, but once they added some sugar it became a different ball game.

While I waited for Hannah to get dressed and walk me to school, I would play with her daughter, Suzanne. We used to play for hours over the garden fence. She was only two. I used to keep her entertained and made her laugh by playing peek-a-boo over the fence. There was a very wobbly wooden table which was tucked into the corner against the fence which I used to climb up and stand on top. The height of the fence once I stood on the table came up to my nose.

When it was time for me to go in for tea she would start crying, telling me to stay and carry on playing. She was so sweet.

When school finished, I don't remember anyone walking me home as I had a key on a chain around my neck to let myself in the house. School finished at about 2.30 in the afternoon and my mum didn't get in from work until four o'clock. My mum would walk in to find me sat crossed legged on the carpet, in front of the television like a good girl. I didn't mind coming home to an empty house as I didn't know whether I should mind or not. It was our house, and my mum would be back soon. It was good to see her and tell her about the exciting things I had done at school. She would then make herself a cup of tea and take herself to bed for an hour or so. "Evie, Mummy is very tired. I am going to bed for a little sleep. Can you wake Mummy up when the clock says half-past five? Then Mummy will wake up and make dinner. When this hand is pointing here, and this hand is pointing here, you come upstairs and tell Mummy." She showed me the clock, pointing to the hands and where they should be positioned before I was allowed to go up and wake her. Sometimes I would get bored and lonely, and I would sneak up and watch her sleeping. She had a unique way of sleeping. I suppose what I am trying to say politely is that she snored – a lot and yet it was comforting to hear. I would creep up quietly and whisper to her, "Mummy, are you going to wake up now?"

She would stir, turn to look at the clock and say, "No, it's not time yet."

I would go back downstairs and watch a bit more television while keeping an eye on the clock. I did keep a constant eye on it as I didn't want to miss the time and wake her up later than I was supposed to, otherwise I would be in trouble. It wasn't so bad.

I enjoyed watching programmes like *Blue Peter*, *Grange Hill*, and *Ivor the Engine*. Eventually, when the clock told me I was now allowed to go and wake my mum, I would run upstairs. My mum always felt refreshed after an hour and a half sleep.

She suffered from epilepsy so it was important she didn't wear herself out too much, otherwise she could have a seizure. I didn't like it when that happened. It was very frightening, and I didn't know what to do.

She always said, "Now, if Mummy has a fit you don't worry, because it will only last a few minutes and then Mummy will be fine. You just stay with Mummy until I wake up. After that, Mummy will be okay."

If you have never seen anyone have an epileptic fit before it can be slightly daunting, especially when you live on your own with your mum. Thankfully, she didn't have them too often and I began to recognise the signs that took place just before she had one. I suppose there isn't a lot you can do when you're four years old.

I would say some things are easier to deal with when you're younger, as you're unaware of all the many things that you could worry about, so you don't worry. When mum had a seizure, all I could do was sit on the floor next to her, or wherever she had fallen. Just be with her, talk to her and keep telling her everything was okay. After several moments of jolting and shuddering she would regain consciousness, her tongue swollen and sore from where she had bitten it. She would ask for an account of what had happened and how long she had been on the floor. After each episode she would be extremely tired and head up to bed for some sleep and rest.

****

64

Going back to when I'm asked, when did you first become a Christian? my reply is, I've always been a Christian. To some extent it is true; my journey may have started at school. Seeds were being sown without me realising it. I can see it clearly now, the stories I heard I believed and wanted the same incredible, miraculous things to happen to me. The prayer we sang in our music lesson, I sang with all my heart; unknowingly was I calling on God to look out for me, protect me even at that young age? Did He see my heart at that moment? I felt as if I was being transported to the villages we were drawing and painting as if they were speaking to me. I wanted "in" then, but I didn't know what "in" was. I believe God heard me and walked with me from then on, without me even knowing that I needed Him.

The Lord's Prayer
Our Father in heaven,
hallowed be your name,
your kingdom come,
your will be done,
on earth as in heaven.
Give us today our daily bread.
Forgive us our sins
as we forgive those who sin against us.
Lead us not into temptation
but deliver us from evil.
For the kingdom, the power,
and the glory are yours
now and forever. Amen.
Matthew 6:9-13, Church of England Version

The Grace

May the grace of the Lord Jesus Christ,
and the love of God,
and the fellowship of the Holy Spirit be with you all,
evermore, Amen
2 Corinthians 13:14 NIV

Chapter 5

Spanish Eyes

May your father and your mother be glad and let her rejoice who gave birth to you. -Proverbs 23:25 NIV

Contrary to what some people would say and think, my mum was a good and courageous woman. After the first initial years of anger and disbelief at my mum's actions and the repercussions it caused my family and me, from the moment she died, I came to love and respect her far more than I did when she was alive.

While Liam was working in London and I was left on my own with many hours to think and ponder and question, I realised lots of things and began to understand and see things from a different point of view. I began to understand, and accept, why my mum was the person she was and why she did the things she did. It wasn't through malice or to be mean, although, yes, sometimes it was to be mean, but if you were to look back and see where she was coming from, then it was understandable. But at the same time, it doesn't make it excusable. It was just the way she was. She meant well and did her best and, it is true, the ones we love the most are sometimes the ones we hurt the most. I still say I wouldn't change a thing, except for the recurring dreams I keep having. Had I known before she died what would come to fruition, I would have spoken out sooner, but then it's all irrelevant now.

My mum was born in Madrid with her father dying just two years later. My Spanish grandmother married my Spanish granddad soon after he had divorced his first wife. Whether it was because of my gran he got divorced I don't know, it is possible. He was an important man, very high ranking in the Spanish army. The sepia photos show him sitting on a horse with rows of medals on his chest and a large sword hanging from his side. He looked important, with black hair neatly slicked back and piercing brown eyes, a man of authority. My mum resembled him a lot, particularly the eyes and the shapes and contours of his brow. There is a Spanish saying, "To those who resemble family, honour is due." My granddad died in a military hospital from a hernia in his stomach.

After his death, mum and her older brother, who was a year and a half older, moved to Barcelona. Barcelona was a city full of work and promise, a good choice for my grandmother trying to bring up two young children. A couple of my grandmother's sisters were already living in the big city, so at least she was not completely alone. Contrary to her expectations, she struggled to find work and found it challenging to provide for two children. It must have been awfully hard in those days.

From a very young age my mum started having epileptic fits and the strain of it all proved too much for my grandmother. She sent my mum to live in a convent and her brother in a priory from the age of three and four years old respectively until they were allowed out at the age of twenty-one. Family could visit their children at weekends and take them out for holidays, but my grandmother rarely did.

Very occasionally she did take them out. It was once every few months for a Sunday stroll, thanks to my great aunt's nagging and her horror at the neglect of my mum and her brother. When they were older my great aunt would take them out for holidays to her house during the summer, for which my mum was always grateful. This would explain my mum's resentment and anger towards her mum;

years locked up in a convent with Catholic nuns, and her brother with monks. My mum used to tell me horrible stories of how the nuns would beat the children and shout at them all the time. She told me how a friend of hers, who she would never forget, died in the shower as she was beaten by nuns. Stories of when she was growing up; being teased and bullied because of her epilepsy. As if losing your father, being abandoned by your mother who never came to visit wasn't bad enough, then to be beaten and bullied throughout your childhood, that would have been demoralising. An upbringing like that could go two ways, you could carry a lot of hurt, pain and become introverted, or it might make you stronger and more determined in life. When mum reached the age of twenty-one, she was able to leave the convent to start a life of her own, but my grandmother didn't agree. The nuns couldn't keep her there forever, so with a little help and persuasion from my great aunts in convincing my grandmother, my mum finally left the convent. Her brother had left for England a year earlier and was settled in this new country and way of life. My grandmother was also contemplating moving abroad.

There was plenty of work on offer and money to be made, so London seemed to be the natural first stop for my mum. London, the big city, bright lights, music and dancing, miniskirts, and fun. A totally different world from the one she had just left behind.

My mother was a very stubborn and determined woman and it stood her in good stead for a lot of things in the future. She always achieved what she wanted when she set her mind to it. Mum loved singing and going dancing, she liked to have fun. I don't mean drinking and getting drunk. She never drank because of the medication she was on for epilepsy.

When the Spanish side of my family first arrived in London, they didn't mind what sort of work they did, as long as they had money coming in. My uncle worked hard as a waiter in a restaurant and was earning good money, good money compared to back in Barcelona, even by today's standards. He had a girlfriend back in Spain and was saving up to go back and get married. He worked his socks off while in London and loved every minute of it. He learnt quite a bit of the lingo while he was working as well. My Spanish grandmother also worked and worked hard. She had a couple of jobs, cleaning people's houses; Spanish speaking people who were very well off. Until one day she found herself a great job as a housekeeper for a lord and lady, who lived in West London. She did all the cooking and managed the house and sometimes their children. I remember being allowed to spend time with my grandmother during the holidays. I had a brilliant time playing with the employer's children's toys. They had a nursery which was full of toys, books, and an array of children's 'transport' which you sat on and got pushed along. My favourite was the milk float. I loved the detail on it; it was a real wow for me who only had a cardboard box, half full of broken toys.

My mum did whatever she could to save some money. She did various cleaning jobs, as well as waitressing, and signed herself up to evening school to learn English. She was there for the long haul.

One day while she was waiting at the bus stop, a black taxi pulled up in front of her, the driver asking if she wanted a lift instead of waiting for the bus. She found the driver particularly good-looking, with a lovely smile. This must have been why my mum accepted the lift.

That is how she met my dad. He was a hunk; it was easy to see why my mum fell for him and him for her, she in her little mini dress, long dark flowing hair, and mysterious dark brown Spanish eyes. She was relatively short, only five foot four, and looked up at this big strong man who was about to whisk her away and live happily ever after, like a knight in shining armour but in a shiny black taxi.

In the wedding photos it looks like everyone is having a lovely time. However not everyone seems to be too pleased. My English side of the family outnumbered the Spanish, and they were all very tall, and imposing; then you can see just a few members on my mother's side, and they are all short and squat, they seem a little uncomfortable. As it happens, I am the tallest on my Spanish side and the shortest on my English side of the family.

My mum was proud and happy being married to my dad for the short time it lasted, and although I don't have all the facts, I would like to think they were very happy during this period, until the day their lives were turned upside down.

To start with, they had me, a beautiful, bouncy baby girl - I have seen the photos! I did look sweet, well-fed, and very content. My mum often told me how I always smiled and laughed with everyone. People would stop her in the street and remark on such a happy baby and what a lovely smile. It's not just me saying this, I'm only going by what I've been told.

To complete the set, my brother was born. How great was that? The perfect family, a beautiful, healthy girl, and now a handsome, healthy baby boy. Isn't that the recipe for a happy family? I was only a year and half old at this point and pleased to have a baby brother to play with. But then fate took a different direction to the one my parents had planned.

The death of my brother had a significant impact on my parents, but when I look back on it now, it is no wonder events took the course they did. My parents divorced soon after his death, due to my father's nervous breakdown. My mum was unable to cope or support him through this time, and this made her feel unsettled, particularly with a very young child around. My dad was in a fragile state. The only thing I knew, along with everyone else, was that my dad would never hurt me. My dad never did hurt me – ever – and never even laid a finger on me. My mum told me that my dad was bipolar, and that he had to have medical treatment and various other barbaric remedies such as electric shock treatment. He was never quite the same after leaving the hospital. My dad was on medication for the rest of his life, the only time he ever had another episode was when his mother died.

Now, nearly fifty years on, I don't believe he had what everyone said he had. Maybe all he needed was some form of counselling after the death of his baby boy, the subsequent breakdown of his marriage and his own mental health. How traumatic must it have been to lose a child in those days? It is traumatic at any time, today parents can go for bereavement counselling and different types of therapy. They are offered help and support which wasn't as readily available all those years ago. And what about my mum? She had lost a son and a husband. Was she offered any help or support? Not to my knowledge. How does a person deal with all the knocks and shunts that life sometimes throws at them?

Now my mum found herself on her own with a young child to support. My dad moved in with his mum and lived only twenty minutes away. He would pick me up every weekend and take me to his new house. I had the best of both worlds.

While I was growing up, mum said how she struggled to get some sort of support from my dad, but he struggled to support himself, let alone me as well. It does sound like I am making excuses for him, but I can only tell you what I know and how I lived. Mum managed several cleaning jobs in London and did what she could to pay the bills and feed us, just like millions of other families out there. I remember going to work with her in my pushchair. She worked for a big bookstore in London, where she used to park me up in a quiet corner where no one would see me and give me some toys to play with while she went off and did the cleaning. I think this must be where I get my love of libraries and bookshops. It was so quiet and cosy in there surrounded by walls and walls of books. Then we would go off to a café where mum did some more cleaning, and I remember my dad coming to meet us one time, and we sat and had a drink and something to eat. One of the favourite jobs my mum did was when she used to work at Donut Diners. While at Donut Diners, she would bring home the most amazing doughnuts that hadn't sold that day. Sometimes the childminder would take her children and me for a walk to the park to play and then on to Donut Diners, in the Arndale Centre so we could drop by and say hello to mum. The array of doughnuts was amazing and, even now, just thinking about them makes my mouth water. The different colours, smells, and toppings would bring a smile to any young child's face.

Once mum returned home from work, she would get dinner ready. For me, a slightly larger than your average-sized meal for a child my age and she ensured I ate every bit of it so I would grow up into "a big, strong, beautiful girl" - her words, not mine. While I ate my pork chops and vegetables, she would sit and eat her tinned sardine in tomato sauce sandwich. She must have really liked them because she ate them every night while I had a cooked meal!

Chapter 6

Silver Screen Heart Throb

Children's children are a crown to the aged,
and parents are the pride of their children
-Proverbs 17:6 NIV

My dad was incredibly special to me and to everyone who knew him. Some people used to call him the gentle giant who wouldn't hurt a fly. He would give you the shirt off his back if you needed it or give his last few pennies to some animal charity, leaving himself with hardly anything. He always wanted to treat you to a Chinese takeaway, and he would put it on his credit card just to see you happy. He lived from week to week, with the dream of winning the football pools or the lottery, and the promise of taking the whole family on a cruise with his winnings. It was the same dream every week. He would ring me three times a day just to say hello and see if I needed anything. As he lived around the corner from me it was easy for him to pop over for a cup of tea. Sometimes we would go for a drive into town, maybe go and have a pint of beer in a nice pub or treat ourselves to a cheese roll from the bakers, followed by a cream cake. We led such a simple life. There was a small group of the older women in the village who would call him up and ask him to drive them to bingo or the hairdressers and then collect them later. He never said no or let them down. If he was lucky, he might get given £5 towards petrol or to treat himself to a pint at the local village club.

In his younger years, he was always the life and soul of any party. Six foot two, dark wavy hair and brown eyes, with a sort of Cary Grant look, all the girls swooned after him. A great guitarist, he used to have his own band back in the early sixties and was set to go on 'Top of the Pops' and about to sign a record deal. None of it came to fruition as he went into the army and was shipped out to somewhere in the Sahara Desert.

The death of my brother and my dad's nervous breakdown was the beginning of the end of my parents' marriage.

In the early seventies electric shock treatment was still regarded as one of the best treatments for my dad's condition. Barbaric when you think about it, coupled with high dosages of drugs. It comes to a point where you don't know who the real person is, and it is hard to determine when they're better or not. "Cure the symptoms, not the cause" or should I say suppress the symptoms, never mind what is causing them? Coming to terms with past events was the problem. Later he was diagnosed as being bipolar and was then prescribed medication for the rest of his life. Once he was released from the hospital, he was a new man, a different sedate man. Most of his get-up-and-go had got up and gone, it had been zapped out of him and the medication didn't help. Now with treatment he was back in his taxi driving around the streets of London. Sometimes in the evenings whilst we watched television a particular celebrity would appear on the screen and my dad would turn to me and say, "He's been in my cab, he has." The number of famous people who have been in the back of my dad's cab!

At the weekend he would pick me up from my mum's and take me to his house. He would come over in his taxi as it was his only mode of transport. I used to sit in the front with him, on the floor where they put the suitcases, and drive through Putney and down to Fulham. Sometimes he'd see someone hailing him down for a ride, and although he was off duty, he would stop. "Where are you heading?" he'd ask, and if it was in the same direction as us, he'd say, "Look, I can take you if you want, but I've got my daughter in the front as we are just going home but I am heading in that direction, so if you want, I'm happy to take you." They always said yes, it was never an issue. My dad just told me to sit very still and keep quiet, which I did, of course.

Sometimes we would drive around London at night with the whole of the city lit up like a beautiful fairground. It was breath taking. Dad would show me all the sights; I was so lucky. One time my dad suggested, "Evie, shall we go to Piccadilly Circus?"

"Oh yes, that would be great. Yes, please, Daddy." I was so excited as I hadn't been to the circus in a long time. I was going to see all the animals and clowns. We parked up and got out of the cab. "Where is the circus, Daddy?" I didn't understand. There wasn't a circus anywhere but lots of cars going around a statue of a man with wings pointing a bow and arrow.

I wondered if the circus was around the corner somewhere as I didn't fancy walking too far. It wasn't until I was slightly older, I realised, it was the place that was called Piccadilly Circus, not that there was a circus there. I was only about five years old. We just walked through the streets looking at all the neon signs, pretty shops and restaurants. It was magical, a little girl in a big city at night-time instead of being tucked up in bed.

Since mum didn't drive and was always working, she and I hardly ever went anywhere exciting, but when I was with my dad my life was another story. We had so much fun driving everywhere, going to fantastic places. We would stop off at a pub, dad would buy me a glass of lemonade and some crisps, and himself a pint of beer. I was so fortunate to have such a great life which was only going to get better.

At the age of seven, my dad and nan had some exciting news to tell me. Exciting for them but devastating for me. Nan sold their house in Fulham; she and Dad were moving back to Hertfordshire where she was born. Nan had had enough of living in London, especially since her divorce, and wanted to go back to the countryside. My initial thought was I wasn't going to see them again. Obviously, this wasn't going to be the case. Of course I was going to see them still and spend weekends with them, just not every weekend as I had done up until now. My dad did his best and picked me up every other weekend. It was a considerable trek from their new place in a lovely village in Hertfordshire to south London; there and back on the same night only to make the same journey again two days later.

Once nan's divorce came through, they moved, and I didn't see them for a few weeks as they were settling down into their new home. My nan described the lovely farms and woods there and how we could go for picnics and play by the river. It sounded charming and idyllic, and it was. When I finally got there, I was impressed, it was so peaceful and calm. There were hardly any cars compared to London.

On Friday nights we all went to the local Social Club where nan played bingo in the hall and Dad would sit with a couple of his friends in the bar area next door. There was a big playing field outside where I used to spend my time running around singing and dancing to the music from the jukebox inside.

As soon as bingo had finished, nan and her newfound friends would come into the bar and have a few more drinks before getting kicked out at closing time. Many a night nan would stroll home which was just across the road and around the corner, a bit worse for wear but very jolly and singing all the way. On more than one occasion I had to stop her from falling into the hedge; I found it hilarious to see her in such a funny state. Once home she would make us all a midnight snack before sending us to bed, usually cheese and crackers, though she would warn me not to eat too much cheese 'it gives you nightmares if you eat it too late at night.' She would then proceed to do the can-can from her armchair and make bets with me to see who could get their leg the highest and the straightest, then continue to have a competition on the floor at doing the splits. For a woman in her seventies, she was phenomenal. Three times a week she would go out to a social club or pub to go singing and dancing. Sometimes she would go and sing to the old folk who were just slightly older than her. She had such a zest for life. She started working part-time at Harrington's, the bakers, a lovely little job making the rolls first thing in the morning. She could make over a hundred rolls, with all their fillings and salad, in an hour. Her morning began at seven-thirty and finished at eleven. She enjoyed it, it was her little bit of pocket money for her cigarettes and her bottle of whisky which she loved.

Soon the summer holidays came. I spent the entire summer with them, and I loved every minute of it. As soon as I awoke, I'd walk up the road and visit my nan at the bakers to say good morning. By then, dad would be at work as an ambulance driver for the local psychiatric hospital and the house would be quiet and still. My nan would welcome me with a warm smile and a quick hug and then send me on my way with a bag full of goodies, usually a sticky bun or two. Perks of the job.

"Are you nearly finished, Nan?"

"Yes, nearly finished. I just have a few more rolls to make as someone came and bought a load in one go, so I'll make sure there are enough to keep them going until lunchtime and then I will be home."

"Okay."

"You go off home now and I'll be along soon. Would you like a roll for your lunch?" Nan enquired.

"What did I have yesterday? That was really nice."

"Cheese salad roll?"

"Yes." Nan hugged me, and I headed back to the house, letting myself in through the back door to wait for her. I thought I would help by doing some housework before she got home, allowing her to sit down and relax for a bit. I busied myself doing some dusting, ran the hoover around the house and did the washing up from breakfast time.

This house was so different from the other one in London. This one was a small compact two-bedroom ground floor maisonette, with a good size kitchen and a lovely garden. When I stayed with nan and dad, I shared nan's bed as there wasn't anywhere else for me to sleep unless I wanted to continue sleeping on the sofa. As it was just her now, I loved sharing a bed with her. Once in bed we would stay awake for hours and shout back and forth to my dad in the next room. We had such a laugh together. I would make her tell me all the stories she had told me so many times before, of the olden days and what it was like growing up during the war. How different everything was now, compared to when she was a child - gross stories of an outside toilet and having to go outside in the freezing cold in winter.

Stories about her growing up in a house full of brothers and sisters and no money, and how people just made do with what they had and were grateful for it. Stories about fishing in the river and getting a clip round the ear, for being naughty. She had such a funny way of relating it all. I thought it was all fantastic and I hung onto her every word.

"Nan, I don't want you to die," I'd say to her, starting to get scared of the thought that one day she wouldn't be here anymore to tell me these wonderful tales.

"Evie, even when I die, I will always be with you, looking out for you, guiding you." She had a special way of saying things. "Him upstairs has a plan for all of us, every single one of us. He has it all written down in His special book."

"Really?" This was amazing. She explained how God always looked after us and was always there to help us with anything we needed.

"You just need to remember to say your prayers every night as I do."

"Do you say prayers every night, Nanny?"

"Every night."

I had never thought of saying prayers every night, not even once a week. I knew about saying prayers at church, but I hadn't taken it very seriously and hadn't given it much thought.

"So how do you pray, Nanny? What do you say?"

"Well, I say thank you for everything I have. I ask for blessings on my family and friends and just talk to God and Jesus." I was intrigued. These seemed to be wise words from a wise woman. "You should always remember to say your prayers, Evie, it's important." She was very insistent and was being serious about it.

Nan and I lay still in the night. We talked till late, and she taught me how to say my prayers, The Lord's Prayer and to say The Grace. I already knew these from school as it was a Church of England school. We always said prayers and went to church regularly, but none of it had really had any effect until that night. Something changed in me. If my nan said God was always listening to me, looking out for me, and had everything written down in a book in heaven, then it must be true. However, I didn't quite realise how true until much later. From that night on, I would say my prayers every single night. Sometimes I would fall asleep before I could start, but now I realise God knows my heart, and it's alright if I don't say them every single night.

The rest of the summer days were spent going for walks along the river and up the lane to the farm to watch the cows being milked. Dad would often come with me, and we would visit the barn where the cows had just given birth. We both loved seeing the new-born calves. They were so cute.

****

One day Jesus was praying in a certain place. When he finished, one of his disciples said to him, "Lord, teach us to pray, just as John taught his disciples."

He said to them, "When you pray, say: "'Father, hallowed be your name, your kingdom come. Give us each day our daily bread. Forgive us our sins, for we also forgive everyone who sins against us. And lead us not into temptation.' -Luke 11:1-4 NIV

Chapter 7

Spanish World Cup 1982

*Then you will call on me and come and pray to me,
and I will listen to you.*
- Jeremiah 29:12 NIV

Valentine's Day, Saturday 14th February 1982, London Victoria
Coach Station. The coach was due to depart at 10 a.m. The smell of
diesel fumes lingered in the air. The smell was making me feel slightly
travel sick, and we hadn't even left yet. As a 10 year old, I was
apprehensive and excited at the same time. Saying goodbye to my dad
and nan the night before had been heart-wrenching. I couldn't bear
to leave them. All those emotions exposed in the middle of a
Kentucky Fried Chicken restaurant in Tooting, of all places. I held
them both with all my might with tears streaming down my face. I
didn't want to let go of them. I don't recall ever feeling that much
sadness before that moment of saying goodbye. Nan kept trying to
reassure me they would be out to visit me as soon as I had settled into
my new home. They would book a flight and come on holiday in the
summer. My mum, also in tears, dragged me away from the emotional
scene, unable to take much more. Seeing nan and dad in tears made
me feel even worse.

Today was a new day, a new life. I enjoyed travelling by coach,
being high up gives you a better view out of the large windows as you
take in the everchanging scenery from one country to the next.

I remembered the times we went on holiday to Spain it was
always by coach; it was the cheapest way to travel. We stayed with my

uncle and aunt in Barcelona. Those were fantastic holidays. I couldn't believe how we were allowed to stay up and play in the street until two o'clock in the morning along with everyone from the whole neighbourhood sitting outside, chatting, and enjoying the cooler night air. Around about 9 p.m., my aunt would come downstairs into the street with a big baguette filled with my favourite Spanish omelette. All the children from the block running around playing without a care in the world. You could understand why people came out so late as it was too hot during the day. In the afternoon we stayed indoors until it cooled down, with the roller blinds partway down to shield the apartments from the heat of the Spanish summer.

Sleeping was always a problem. Every window was left open in the hope that a slight breeze would pass through the tiny gaps of the blinds. All you could hear was the relaxing sound of crickets and men down at the bar talking and laughing, their voices travelling through the stillness of the warm summer night.

In the morning, my two cousins and I would be rudely awakened by my uncle shouting through the apartment. If he was awake, because he had gone to bed early, then everyone else should be awake regardless of what time they had gone to bed.

My aunt would be busy filling the cool box with sandwiches, crisps and bottles of orange and lemon Fanta. Sundays were made for spending on the beach. 7.30 a.m., we all had to be up, washed and ready to get into pole position along with the rest of the city who also thought it would be a good idea to head to the coast. There was only one road which led to it, and no one wanted to get stuck in what is known in Spanish as *"La Caravana"*, essentially one long traffic jam. You could be stuck in traffic for over an hour with no air-conditioning. All six of us were cramped in the five-seater car. I sat on mum's lap with my two cousins squashed up next to us, - such great memories.

I settled down into my allocated seat on the coach next to the window, loaded with a bag full of comics, a word search magazine and a couple of jigsaw puzzles to keep me amused for the thirty-hour drive to Barcelona where our new life awaited us. We were going to live like royalty, Mum said, and she was never going to have to work again. She had sold our house in south London and with the difference in property value and the exchange rate, financially, we were set for life.

When we arrived in Barcelona, my uncle came to meet us. He took us back to his house where we stayed for a couple of days while mum spent a lot of time making phone calls, to whom and about what I had no idea. "Right, Evie, today is the day we're going to stay in our new house." I was so excited, I wondered what it was going to be like. "We need to go and see the man from the agency. He has found us a lovely house."

We arrived at a little town by the sea, close to Gerona, but mum couldn't get hold of the man we were supposed to be meeting. We turned up at his house and were greeted by his wife. It was a beautiful house with a swimming pool and lovely furniture, with carefully coordinated décor and design. This man was obviously very rich. In the lounge area were big comfy sofas covered with brightly coloured velvet cushions. A ceramic cheetah stood proudly in the corner of the living room, nearly as tall as me. I was told to go out into the garden and play with his daughter, who was about the same age as me. I watched her as she splashed about in her swimming pool, teasing her German Shepherd Dog who watched protectively over her from the side. I hoped our house was going to be as lovely as this one. It felt homely, full of personal knick-knacks and lots of beautiful family framed photographs placed on an expensive wooden sideboard. In our old house in London everything was basic. We had a couple of empty bookshelves where the record player lived, a school photo of me plus a couple of odd ornaments for decoration. A cuckoo clock hung on the wall. There was nothing special about our sofa, apart from it opened into a sofa bed. Mum and I would sometimes sleep on it at the weekend while watching a late-night horror film together.

This house looked like a rock star lived in it, and I so wanted it to be mine. I made a mental note that one day I would have one just like it, and if not, very similar.

For some reason, I could hear mum's voice rising, which was something she did quite often, especially when she was speaking in Spanish. I went into the house to see what was happening. "Are you alright, Mummy?"

"Yes, it's all okay, darling. When I spoke to the man on the phone, he said the house was going to be ready for us, now he says it's not available anymore! However, he has another house where we can stay for the time being." She seemed very frustrated and somewhat deflated. At least we had been offered somewhere to stay. We left the man's house and headed back into the centre of town. It was a lovely walk back along the *Paseo*, with the beach to our left and a selection of bars and restaurants to the right. Mum was ready for a coffee and a sit down while she gathered her thoughts. We surveyed the choice of bars and chose one that didn't seem too expensive or upmarket. We just wanted an ordinary no-fuss bar to sit for a while. We picked one and went inside. Mum ordered me a Coke and a doughnut, she had a coffee and lit herself a cigarette. I sat there quietly drinking my drink and eating my delicious sugary treat.

Everywhere we went, mum striked up conversations with people. Everyone was so friendly and cheerful. We decided we would come back later and have lunch in the same bar as the owners were lovely. First, we had to go and visit our new accommodation. We turned away from the *Paseo* and headed down the back roads. As we turned down a smelly old side street, I felt confused. "Mummy, what are we doing down here? The nice houses are down the other end of the road where we've just come from." I was still thinking of the young girl with her swimming pool and gorgeous German Shepherd.

"We're just going to stay here for a little while, just a couple of days."

We stopped outside an old building which had seen better days. Bags of decaying rubbish lay outside, and the walls were stained with urine where all the local dogs had marked their territory. We walked into a narrow, dingy entrance with bits of plaster falling off the walls. There was a smell of dampness in the air, and it turned out these were flats! This was where we were going to be staying, on the first floor in a flat with only one bedroom, so I'd have to sleep with mum. There was a tiny living room with no TV and an even smaller kitchen.

"Mummy, we're not going to stay here, are we?" I held on to my mum's arm, dreading the prospect that this was going to be our new home. I could smell lunch being cooked by the surrounding neighbours. You could hear everything they were saying.

"I don't want to stay here." Tears began to roll down my face. I was hot and tired, and still feeling sensitive from having said goodbye to dad and nan. "You said we were going to live in a nice house better than the one we had in England. I want to go home back to England and see Daddy. I miss Daddy."

"Evie, it's okay. This is our home for now. We are only going to be staying here for a couple of days and then the man is going to find us a lovely house to live in, you'll see." I relented. If it was only temporary, then it would be alright while we waited for things to get sorted. Mum hugged me and consoled me as much as she could.

We put our bags down, had a quick wash, then went back to the bar around the corner for some lunch. My uncle would come over the next day with the rest of our essential things and suitcases.

First thing Monday morning we went to the local town hall to find me a school. Mum was hoping to find an English-speaking school or at least one that taught English. She was handed a list of the various schools in the local area, ranging from Roman Catholic schools to the general State school. The Catholic schools she crossed off the list straight away because of her childhood experiences in the convent, that was the last place she was going to send me. We spent the morning walking around the whole town visiting the other potential schools. After visiting three schools, my mum was getting to the end of her tether. The schools wouldn't accept me because I couldn't speak a word of Spanish. Mum was incredulous. She couldn't believe her ears. "So, you're telling me, if a foreigner comes here to live you will not let them in just because they don't speak Spanish?" Good on you Mum, you tell them. How else was I supposed to learn? "So, what you're saying is my daughter just doesn't go to school? What a backward country this is. I am ashamed to call this my country. How backwards can you be?" She was going for it now, shouting at the headmaster. She left fuming and throwing abuse.

I hated staying where we were. At night-time you could hear the neighbours and their conversations, their chairs scraping along the floor and their TVs blaring. A young couple in the flat below us decided to practice the guitar every night and play flamenco music. I tossed and turned with frustration trying to get to sleep. Mum decided to go downstairs to ask them to try and keep the noise down but ended up staying with them for a while having a can of Coke. At least they did keep the noise down.

Towards the end of the week, we moved to Barcelona into a rented three-bedroom apartment. It had a large living area and a large balcony which looked out onto a children's play park just in front. It was great. I spent most of my time playing outside and making new friends. I was the new kid on the block who was English and couldn't speak Spanish. The local kids took pride in teaching me their language which when at home I would recite to my mum and then get a smack for it. They were teaching me all the swear words first and thought the conversational part should come later.

I was accepted into a school which was a bit of a trek from where we lived. You had to cross a large bridge beneath which a community of gypsies lived. It was fascinating to see how they were living. They lived in shacks with corrugated iron roofs, battered old windows. Little toddlers covered in dirt run barefoot around a dirty, dusty track. Some of the children were trouserless, bare behinds, and munching on bits of bread. They seemed happy and content. How could they live like that? I asked myself. It was a real shantytown.

The school wasn't bad. I was told to sit at the back of the class and copy text all day long from a textbook. This way, I would learn how to write in Spanish, although I had no idea what I was writing about. I'm sure the teachers knew what they were doing.

One day when I arrived home from school mum greeted me at the front door, asked me how my day was and before I could walk into the living room I was promptly introduced to a man, her new boyfriend. I didn't know mum was seeing anybody. I had no idea she had made any new friends.

A strange man was standing in the living room. I wouldn't say he was attractive or even good-looking. There was nothing special about him. I couldn't see what she saw in him. He had a round face and a bulbous nose and slightly bulging eyes. He was cheery enough though.

"Evie, I want you to meet Carlos. We have been out for a couple of drinks, and he is a very nice man, so I want you to be very nice and kind to him and show him what a good girl you are," she said in a whisper and obviously in English. There was also the underlying tone of "don't mess this up for me". The man didn't understand a word she was saying. I knew what I had to do, at the same time thinking, I'd better not mess this up for her. So, like a good girl, I went over and shook his hand, and I spoke to him in the little Spanish I had learnt so far.

"Oh, by the way, another letter from your dad arrived today." She handed me the envelope.

"Wow! Thanks, Mum." I took it eagerly. I looked forward to receiving letters from England. Nan wrote more than dad, but she wrote for both of them as he never knew what to say. Nan was an excellent letter writer, and she would write pretty much every week, giving me the lowdown on what was going on with the family and in the village. I loved reading them, and I'd read them over and over.

"When you have finished reading it, and you have had your snack, why don't you go downstairs and play for a while?"

"Okay, Mum." This roughly translated as "make yourself scarce." I knew I would be in trouble if I ruined anything for her and I didn't want it to be my fault.

A couple of weeks later we moved again to a different area entirely. This time mum had bought somewhere of our own. It was a flat on the twelfth floor, just outside Barcelona on the Gran Via. It felt a bit scary living so high up, looking down over the balcony. It was nice enough though, and she'd chosen some nice furniture to go in it. My new school was just downstairs on the ground floor of the building opposite. The school was part of the flats and had been converted for the local children. It was a private school and mum paid a lot of money for me to go there, but in hindsight, I have no idea why she paid them a single peseta. It would have been shut down if today's standards were anything to go by.

I was in a classroom of forty-one students with rows of desks back-to-back against each other. You weren't allowed to leave your desk unless you were busting to go to the toilet, which was an experience in itself. There were five classrooms, all on the same level with an average of forty students to each class. We all shared one stinking toilet which lacked a toilet seat, there was no toilet paper and just one sink to wash your hands. There was never any soap or towels to dry your hands, and it always stank of urine. Unfortunately for one classroom, they were right next door to the toilet. The poor teacher couldn't bear to have the classroom door open - which was necessary during the summer months, to try to let some sort of air in - due to the stench. It could get hot and stuffy in the summer with just one small window to open. There was no air-conditioning, just your textbook, exercise book, the blackboard and the smell of sweaty bodies and urine.

Usually, when you are in secondary school, it's the students who move from class to class, but in this case, it was the teachers. Morning break time was spent at your desk, eating your mid-morning snack.

There was a big park next door where some of my friends and I used to hang out after school and at weekends. There were five of us who were incredibly close, and we tended to hang out as a gang most of the time. We were like the Famous Five. We went everywhere together.

At weekends we would walk to Montjuic, down to the Ramblas and sometimes visit the stunning cathedral in the Gothic Quarter. I loved visiting the cathedral and having a look around in silence. There was always a certain hush about the place, along with an atmosphere of reverence and expectation. On my first visit, I tried to find Jesus, I was surprised I couldn't see Him anywhere. There were so many little chapels protected behind bars dedicated to dead people. I had no idea who they were, nor did I understand why they had such elaborate shrines. There was a shrine to someone called Luke, Mark, John and lots of others but I couldn't understand why they seemed to be more or just as important as Jesus, whilst He was nowhere to be found. I approached the altar at the front, looking for Him but He wasn't there. Where was the cross with Jesus on it? There was a statue of a beautiful lady dressed in blue, holding a baby, but I wanted to speak to the Man, not the baby. I came to see the Man I prayed to. I started to get a bit concerned, how could you have a church and not have Jesus as the central focus of it? where you can come and pray before Him. Every time I came across a church, I liked to go in, have a look around, say a little prayer, ask for help or just say hello.

My mum was worried I might lose my ability to speak English while living in Spain, so she found an international English-speaking church on the other side of the city. I went there every Sunday on my own and to the youth group on Tuesday evenings. It was fun and I did get to meet English-speaking children my age. I had to get two buses across Barcelona, straight after school, and back again. It got a bit tiresome, especially on the dark winter nights all on my own. I made friends with an American family and their three girls. The parents Sarah and Ted could see that my life wasn't as normal as it could have been, as I spent so much time on my own. They invited me a couple of times to spend the day with them, going out for walks into the countryside and playing at their house. When they found out I was leaving to go back to England for the second time, they gave me a Bible as a gift. Inside of the black leather-bound book, they wrote a treasured message; *"Evie, we love you and pray God's richest blessing on you, from the Roberts family, Sarah, Ted, Julie, Hannah and Emily."*

I never saw them again or know where they live or how to contact them, but I still have that Bible and use it now more than ever, thirty-five years on. I do wonder where they are now, as I'd like to say thank you.

Whilst in the Church I continued searching in all the shrines and then, towards the exit was a section set back to the side, off the main area, with benches and there He was. I had found Him. I found a spot not too close to the other people who had also come to pray. I didn't want to encroach on their space. Some people were kneeling, some were sitting. You could see a couple of ladies crying as they prayed, others just stared towards the cross in silence, some had their head in their hands as if in desperation. I stilled myself and looked up at Him. I'm sure He heard my usual prayers, but just in case, I was here now, right in front of Him. "Dear God, please look after my dad and nan in England…" I sat there and prayed about so many different things. "And for my mum, please help her to get lots of work…" There was so much I wanted to ask Him and tell Him. "Please? if it's possible to visit my dad in the holidays, please keep me safe when I fly over there and be close to me, you know how much I hate flying." They were just simple, everyday prayers of a twelve-year-old. I poured out my heart. I was having a one-way conversation with Him, I kept going with tears rolling down my face. I had no idea why I was crying. I knew He could fix things, make them better.

After praying, I just sat there in silence for a while, enjoying the space I was in. Eventually, I thought I had better go and find the others as they would be waiting for me outside. As I stepped outside, I winced at the brightness, while my eyes adjusted to the sunlight. We followed our usual route and continued down *Las Ramblas* to the statue of Christopher Columbus, who stood pointing the way to America. We felt so grown up and independent buying ourselves cans of Coke and bags of pipas, (sunflower seeds in their shells) a popular snack in Spain. We would go and chill on a bench and spend most of the time chatting before heading back home again. We did so much walking, and we never thought anything of it. I don't feel I could do it now. Barcelona was our playground. We did what we wanted and went where we wanted with just a couple of hundred pesetas in our pockets. If we weren't off wandering the back streets of Barcelona, you could find us sitting on a bench at the bottom of the block of flats happily reflecting on life. Life was good.

Mum seemed to be getting on very well with Carlos, and he was an okay kind of guy. Soon after he moved in with us, she bought him a new car, and for our summer holiday we drove along the coastal road south as far as Cartagena. It was a slow, relaxed drive with no agenda and no hurry. We made lots of stops on the way and stayed in quaint little bed and breakfasts, eating in different restaurants every day. We had a great time. Each town and village we stopped at had something different to offer, from beautiful scenery to golden beaches. After a couple of hours driving, if we were feeling too hot, we would park the car up next to the sea and jump in the water to cool down. If we came across a town we liked the look of, we'd look for somewhere to stay and just soak up the atmosphere. There was such a buzz going on in the summer of 1982 throughout the whole of Spain. At the time, I didn't quite understand why. The cities of Valencia and Alicante were full of traffic. People on the streets and massive billboards with a cartoon orange holding a football on nearly every street corner. Televisions and cheering emanated out of bars. The football World Cup was being held in Spain and matches were being played what seemed to be all day long. Cars drove through cities blowing their horns trying to get from one end to the other. The cartoon orange had been designed and selected to be Spain's mascot; he even had his own cartoon series. Spain was pulsating.

We drove through beautiful countryside and visited a village called Cuevas, where people lived in caves. It was an eye-opening adventure for a young girl. I loved seeing all the new places, meeting new people, and trying all the different foods and tastes. I would go off by myself and explore while mum and Carlos sat in the bar and relaxed. We stopped at a fantastic hotel in a place called Benidorm. This was supposed to be our main destination. I was so excited I couldn't wait to arrive. Every day I was learning more Spanish and looked forward to practising it on the staff in the hotel and couldn't wait to swim in the hotel swimming pool. When I saw the town on the horizon, it looked exciting, like something out of a film, with a dozen high-rise buildings and rows and rows of restaurants, bars, and shops. I wanted to immerse myself in the Spanish culture and learn from it. Unfortunately, to my surprise and disappointment, when we finally arrived and checked in to our hotel, everyone spoke English.

The place was full of English pubs serving English food and beer. I felt cheated. It was as if I had arrived back in England but with more sunshine. There was a disco every night in the hotel where I'd dance the night away dressed to impress with my brand-new holiday clothes. I was looking good, a confident girl having a fabulous time in my own company. Mum would get up for some of the dances and have a boogie with me then soon returned to her seat so as not to leave Carlos alone too long. I would love to make that trip again. I know it would be hard to replicate as it was nearly thirty-eight years ago, and the construction and development that has gone on since then is beyond belief. What once was a lovely little fishing village has now been swallowed up by the continuous growth of English and other foreign ex-pats buying abroad and moving out there.

After two weeks of leisurely travelling down the coast, we turned the car around and headed for home. Mum decided we were going to move into Carlos' apartment, which was sitting empty. They had talked about it and concluded it would be a good idea. Mum bought new furniture and furnished the entire flat and paid for all the decorating. While we lived with Carlos, she would rent out our flat. I stayed on at the same school but had a half an hour walk back and forth four times a day, with my super heavy school bag on my shoulder but it wasn't a problem.

Chapter 8

Salmon from Scotland

*For our light and momentary troubles are achieving for us an
eternal glory that far outweighs them all.*
- 2 Corinthians 4:17 NIV

Summer turned to autumn, then winter and before we knew it
summer was fast approaching again. For my summer holidays, I was
able to visit my dad and nan in England. Nan paid for my flight, and
I travelled as an unaccompanied minor with Spain's national airline. I
didn't enjoy flying on my own with no one to talk to or to tell me
what was happening whilst flying through turbulence. I would sit in
my seat, holding on to the armrests for dear life, with my seatbelt
securely fastened throughout the entire flight. Dad would be at the
other end to receive me, and we would drive back to his house. I loved
coming back to England after having spent all the time surrounded
by concrete buildings, grey pavements, and traffic fumes. I missed
being in the countryside. I missed the greenness of the fields, the
flowing rivers and walking for miles along the country lanes and farm
tracks. Most of all, I missed my nan. I was welcomed with arms
opened wide and a big smile. It was so lovely to be back in the peace
and quiet. Nan would sometimes prepare me a little picnic and I
would stick it in my bag and go down to one of my favourite spots
down by the river.

Since moving out of London, dad now worked as an ambulance
driver, driving psychiatric patients from one hospital to another, even
sometimes for days out to the beach. Every so often, he would take

me to work with him. I would follow him closely when he went on to the wards. A lot of the wards were locked for security reasons and you had to wait a couple of minutes until you were allowed in. There were a lot of weird-looking people walking around the place with vacant stares and mumbling to themselves. Some would come up to me to say, "hello," and I would cling on to my dad's arm for reassurance. "It's okay. They won't harm you; they just want to say hello."

My dad was very good with all the patients. He would often take them sweets and treats. "Hello, Robert," a patient would say chuckling to himself without stopping to wait for any acknowledgement. I found it all quite frightening.

You could hear nurses shouting at some of the patients, trying to get their attention, so that they would do what was being asked of them. Some of them just sat in big, tall armchairs, staring vacantly at the television. I hated going onto the wards. One summer dad took me with him to a holiday seaside resort not far away, with an ambulance full of patients. I hadn't realised at the time they were going to be coming with us. They were going to be spending the weekend there with their carers and dad was to bring them back a couple of days later.

When dad got home from work, and we had finished having dinner, he would shout out, "Who fancies a trip to Southend?"

"What, now?" Nan would ask in surprise.

"Yes, come on, let's get in the car and go. We'll be there in an hour and a bit. It's only 5.30 p.m. If we go now, we can be there for seven." My dad was excited.

"Yeah, let's go, Dad. Come on. It'll be fun." I so was excited by this show of spontaneity.

"You go. I'm going to stay here and watch *Coronation Street*."

"Oh, come on, Nan. It'll be fun."

"No, no," said Nan holding her hand up. "You go on and have some fun. Besides, I'm tired, I was up early this morning for work."

"Okay, we won't be late," said Dad grabbing his car keys and wallet.

"Don't forget you've got work in the morning, Robert," Nan reminded him, hinting he shouldn't be too late back. Once there we had a couple of goes in the amusement arcades and bought some sweets. I always chose a bag of honeycomb. I hate, however, how it sometimes gets stuck in your teeth. We then headed to the nearest pub. A little trip like this was just a nice change of scenery.

A couple of weeks into my four-week holiday nan called me into the living room to sit down and have a chat. "Evie, come and sit down here next to me." I went and sat down where I always sit, by the fire on the floor leaning against her armchair in front of the television. It wasn't a large room. It was cosy and comfortable. Enough room for a three-seater sofa, a coffee table with an armchair either side facing the TV, looking out onto the garden. Nan loved to sit and watch the birds go about their business and watch her washing blowing in the wind. "There is something about fresh clean washing hanging out on the line blowing in the wind," she always said. "It's very satisfying."

"Evie, you like it here, don't you?"

"Yes, you know I do. I love it here."

"Well, how would you like to stay and live here?" she asked tentatively.

"What, here with you and Dad?"

"Yes. Would you like to?"

"Where would I go to school?"

"You would go to the school in the town because the one in the village is about to close. You would have to get the bus with the rest of the children."

"But what about Mum? What would she say? She would be ever so upset if I came over here to live." I started to worry about my mum and her feelings and how she wouldn't agree to any of this.

"Well, you see, I have been speaking to your mum because apparently she has split up from her boyfriend, Carlos, is it?" I nodded, wondering what was coming next. "She has kicked him out, and she says she has no money left to look after you and she thought it would be much better if you stayed here and lived with us."

I couldn't believe my ears. Yes, it would be great to stay here and live in England, but what about my poor mum? She must be devastated. She wouldn't have taken the decision lightly. I had to phone her and see how she was. "I don't know how we'll cope because I only have my pension and your dad doesn't have a lot of money, but we'll manage somehow. If you want to stay with us, you're more than welcome." Again, I was excited and bewildered at the same time. I had to call my mum.

I could sense my mum's pain over the phone. She was ever so upset but tried not to show it. She had spent all her money on Carlos and didn't have a penny left. She was going to have to find a job which would be difficult as she was a woman the wrong side of forty and in a Spanish man's world. Women once married were expected to stay at home to look after their husband, children, and the home. Very rarely did they go back to work. Jobs were very hard to come by. Employers would ask for qualifications even for a job which involved cleaning toilets, and with mum's epilepsy, she found herself in a very awkward situation.

I didn't return to Spain at the end of my holiday. Instead, I started school in St. Albans, and on my first day, I was pleasantly surprised.

The school to me seemed as if it was out of an American film like *Grease*, compared to the small school I was attending in Spain. This school was huge. It had so many different types of classrooms and laboratories used for biology, physics and chemistry. There was a dedicated art department, a metalwork and woodwork area, a department for sewing and a kitchen full of ovens and sinks for cookery. I didn't know any of these hands-on subjects even existed. All we did in my other school was sit at our desk for six hours a day memorising whatever it said in the book. This school even had its own swimming pool and a playing field, it was fantastic. I wrote regularly to my mum, telling her of the different things I had been up to. I sent her a couple of photos of me standing proud in my school uniform and one in my PE kit ready to play hockey. I'd never heard of hockey before. It was a whole new adventure which I relished.

My new best friend, Samantha, lived next door to my aunt. We had met many years ago when we were about three or four years old at Christmas, the few times I had accompanied my dad when he had come up from London to visit my aunt. We soon became inseparable. She would wait for me every morning at 7.45, and we would get the bus to school together. At break time we waited for one another to finish our lessons and then we would hang out together. We saved each other seats at the dinner table and then at the end of the day we caught the bus home. Sometimes in the summer we would walk home to save our bus fare so we could spend it on sweets instead. Saturdays we'd go into town shopping and then at night hire the scariest video we could find from Video Junction, buy a can of Coke and a packet of crisps. We spent Sunday afternoons in my nan's bedroom eating freshly made rock cakes and experimenting with nan's very limited make-up selection whilst listening to the charts on the radio.

The year went by so quickly and the summer holidays were fast approaching.

"Evie, I miss you so much," said my mum one day over the phone. "I have a new job now, and I'm making some money. You can come back to live with me again. Everything will be fine" pleaded my mum over the phone.

"Evie, your mum wants you to return to Barcelona to be with her. What do you think? She misses you a lot," Nan said. With this new situation I didn't know what to think. I couldn't leave my mum if she wanted me to go back to her. She was my mum after all, and she said everything would be alright now she had a new job and money coming in. Carlos wasn't there anymore so it would be just her and me again like it used to be. I did miss her, I was her little girl, she needed me.

"Evie, you know you will always have a home here and we love you very much," my nan said reassuringly, but it was decided. I was to return to Spain. I had lost a year in my Spanish school which meant I would have to repeat a year. All my friends who I was with before would now be in the year above me. But that was okay as I knew I wouldn't be able to pass any of my exams anyway, had I continued with them. It was hard to say goodbye to dad and nan as it always was, but it wasn't as bad as the first time. I was older now, more mature. I was now twelve going on thirteen. I knew the Christmas holidays were on the way and there was always the option of dad coming out or me going back.

I was a different girl arriving in Spain to the one that left. I was more independent. I hadn't had mum to tell me what to do or how to do it.

She wasn't there to shout at me when I did the slightest thing wrong. Equally, she hadn't been there to give me loads of cuddles and kisses every night and tell me how beautiful I was. I didn't get that at my dad's. Nan and dad weren't as touchy-feely as mum was, they didn't tell you several times a day how much they loved you like mum did. This wasn't a problem, I knew they loved me, but they weren't the type to go shouting about it. I feel that this also influenced me. I didn't want to be kissed and cooed over all the time as if I were a baby, especially in public. Mum would get upset by this; I was no longer her little girl. I had my own opinions, my likes, and dislikes, but I was never allowed to express them. My view was always wrong.

Mum's new job was working in a big outdoor trading estate, selling cigarettes throughout the night to lorry drivers who had been travelling day and night. Lorries packed with fish from Scotland and fruit and vegetables from the south of Spain, freshly transported and ready for the market traders to come in the early hours to buy their stock for the day.

It was a large industrial zone where lots went on during the day and night. There was a huge restaurant where the drivers could go and eat a good meal at a special rate and relax for a bit. Mum had a table in the corner selling tobacco, and within a few weeks she started selling lottery tickets. She began work at about eight o'clock at night and would return home at about four o'clock in the morning, sometimes five. I would be left on my own, which wasn't a problem for me. I would make my dinner, finish my homework, and then take myself off to bed when I felt tired, knowing I had to get up early in the morning making sure I didn't wake up my mum.

Mum didn't mind working there as it got her out of the house, and it was a way of making new friends. The money wasn't bad, but it wasn't great either. She didn't get paid a wage but only made a profit on what she sold. She had to buy all her own stock in the first place, put a mark up on it and then she kept the difference. She had to sell a lot of cigarettes to make anything worthwhile. It was just enough to get by day by day.

At weekends I would go down with her on the bus, and we would have dinner together in the restaurant. As usual, she introduced me to all the bar and restaurant staff. Later in the evening, she would take me across the road to where the nightclub was. In the entrance, there were lots of photographs of half-naked women dancing and made up in cabaret-style dress with giant feathered fans and sequined thongs.

I felt a bit embarrassed, but this was the place where the men came to relax and unwind after their meal before going back to their lorries to sleep for the night. My mum shuffled me along, but there were so many different questions going on in my head, wondering what exactly went on here at night. Still, it did seem exciting, and everyone was so friendly and welcoming. Mum introduced me to some of the girls backstage. "Evie, I want you to meet Sonia. This is my friend, the one I told you about in the letters. She is the one who always makes me smile when I am sad because you were in England. She is so kind to me."

"Hello. Nice to meet you." We greeted each other with two kisses on the cheek.

"Oh, isn't she lovely? How beautiful, how polite. Your mum has told me so much about you. Sometimes we sit here, and all she talks about is my daughter this, my daughter that. She missed you so much. You can tell how happy she is now you're back." Sonia was a lovely friendly person, young and beautiful. "Are you going to stay and watch the show?"

"I don't think so. She will have to go back home soon. It's late, and she isn't eighteen yet. She shouldn't be here. I'll get in trouble if the manager finds us." We said our goodbyes and mum led me away from the club, as we left, we walked past a tiny little cloakroom where there was a small table and chairs. "This is where I work late at night, selling cigarettes. I sit and I listen to the music. Most of it is in English and the girls always ask me to translate the words. But you know me, I'm no good at it."

Once outside in the night air, it was peaceful. Most of the bays were full of lorries from all over Europe. "Oh, let's go and see if my friend is here. He sometimes gives me some salmon; it comes all the way from Scotland." Salmon, all the way from Scotland? I thought to myself. That's a long way away and then to sell it here in Spain. "He isn't here yet. We'll come back later." She was so excited to be able to introduce me to all her friends as she had been talking about me every night and probably boring them to bits as well. I too was excited for her as I could see how happy she was.

Finally, at about 11.30 p.m., it was time for me to go home. "Right, you go in this taxi and the driver will take you home. Go straight to bed when you get in."

"Okay." She put me in a taxi, told the driver where to take me and to make sure I made it into the building safely. She knew the taxi driver as he regularly picked up from the estate and had driven my mum home on various occasions. "I will be home soon. Okay?"

"Okay Mum, see you in the morning," and with a kiss goodnight, I was in a taxi at midnight going through the back streets of Barcelona. As mum worked all night, when Saturday mornings came, I would have to get up early to avoid the crowds and the heat and go with my trolley to the indoor market to do the weekly shop. It was a bit of a walk, but I was never in a hurry. Mum would give me a shopping list and tell me which stallholders to go to. We bought the same things pretty much every week, so it wasn't hard to remember. We never went to a supermarket as there weren't many. We never bought processed food, breakfast cereals or sauces in a jar, as everything was prepared from scratch.

It was everyday simple home cooking. I would buy a selection of meats, lots of vegetables and fruit, and then from the cake stall a bag of *magdalenas*, or little mini croissants, that would last the whole week. These were for breakfast. Before school, children would have a big glass of the chocolate milk drink, *Cola Cao*, and a couple of fairy cakes dunked in it, and then again as a snack when they got home. Back at home, after putting all the shopping away while mum slept, my next task was housework. It was the same every day. Make all the beds, dust, sweep, mop and tidy throughout the whole apartment. It didn't take long, but it was done every morning religiously before preparing lunch. Lunch tended to be the main cooked meal of the day. On an evening people would typically sit and have a sandwich or a salad with some cold meats or an omelette. It made sense. It is not good to go to bed on a full stomach, especially as they ate so late at night. Once I had finished laying the table, I'd wake mum up with a nice cup of tea. Lunch would soon be ready.

Saturday afternoons also had a set routine. After washing up all the lunch things and cleaning down the kitchen, mum and I would sit and watch the three o'clock news followed by the children's cartoon about a bumblebee called Maya. As soon as it finished, I would go and have a wash and put on my best clothes, a splash of perfume, make sure my hair looked good, and then I'd go downstairs and meet my friends.

We would hang out for about three hours and then head back to our homes in time for tea. When I got back to the apartment, mum would be busy getting ready to go to work, hair up in rollers, plucking her eyebrows and putting on her make-up. Mum loved to dress up, and she looked so gorgeous when she had all her make-up on. She liked to wear nice clothes when going out and she made an effort. As she was relatively short, to compensate she would wear high heels that would clack along the granite floor tiles of the apartment. With her nails painted red and matching red lipstick, she looked stunning.

"Okay, I'm off to work now. How do I look?"

"You look lovely, Mum. I hope you sell lots of cigarettes."

"I'll try. Tomorrow, shall we go to the Ramblas for a coffee?"

"Yes, that would be nice. Can we go and see all the animals?"

"Yes. Why not? Right, I better go, or I'll be late. See you in the morning. Be good."

After a few weeks, work slowed down for some reason and mum wasn't making as much money as she hoped, so much so she was struggling to make enough money to buy the tobacco in the first place. Money was becoming short again.

"Evie, I've been talking to a girl in the club, and she has told me about this fantastic job where I can make lots of money for us."

"Sounds good. Where is it?"

"There is a problem, it's in another town about two hours away from here. I will have to stay there during the week and come home on Sundays. You will be alright here on your own, won't you? I could ask Eva's mum if you could go to her house for lunch and dinner and then you could come here to sleep at night."

"Yes, I suppose it sounds alright if you're going to make some money over there. When would you go and come back?"

"I would go on Tuesday and come back on Sunday morning. I could ask Eva's mum if Eva could sleep here with you at night."

"I suppose it would be fun. We're together all the time anyway."

"Well, let's see what she says first," Mum spoke to Eva's mum and arranged a fee to pay her for the extra food and cooking. Her mum was happy for us to stay at mine after we had our dinner as long as we made sure we had finished our homework. This was going to be exciting, I thought.

Mum left, and it was tranquil around the flat without her. I was at school all week and the time went by fast. Everything seemed to be okay. I was on my own most of the time, but I still missed my nan and dad and living in the countryside, I was beginning to miss my old English school. Mum had been working for a couple of months, and she was doing well, bringing home money, and always leaving some so I could do some shopping during the week, but when she was at home, she was always shouting at me or telling me off for things that weren't my fault. She still wanted me to be her little girl and do exactly what she told me to do. I was growing up and changing all the time, but she was never there to see it happen. The more I grew up, the more we would argue. "You ungrateful girl. You horrible girl, everything I have done for you. I go out to work for you, and do you say thank you? You are just like your father. You don't appreciate anything I do for you. You only love your bloody dad and nan; you don't care about your poor old mum." She went on and on, the same script, the same words. "I work all my life and for what? I bring you up on my own with no help from your father, and you don't care."

"All I said was that I miss England a little bit. It's different there. Here it's all blocks of flats. There's no greenery and the school's different."

"You never care about me. I was brought up by the nuns and I have looked after you like I was never looked after. And this is how you treat me? Your dad never gave me a penny to look after you. I should have locked you up with the nuns earlier like my mum did to me. I should have locked you up until you are twenty-one." I was no longer listening. It was easier that way.

"I could have gone and had a life, you ungrateful person, you wicked, evil girl."

She was going off on one like she sometimes did and blamed me for everything or would scream at me for something that had happened by accident. "You did it on purpose, didn't you?"

"I didn't, Mum, honestly. It just fell off the table."

"You saw it was going to fall off. Why didn't you stop it?"

"I couldn't stop it. I couldn't reach it."

"You did it on purpose like everything you do. You are crazy, just like your father. He's crazy, and you are just like him." And then twenty minutes later came the next bit. "Well?"

"Well, what?" I'd ask despondently.

"Are you not going to say sorry? You could at least say sorry." I managed to build up some sort of courage to reply.

"Why? Every time I go to say sorry for anything you say it's too late and that I should have said it earlier." Then off she would go again, screaming and shouting at me for not having gone up to her after she had been yelling at me, to tell her how sorry I was for something I didn't do. In the past, I would generally have succumbed to this theatrical performance, but I couldn't hold it back any longer. I had to stand up for myself. I never argued with anyone, the arguing and shouting at home was wearing me down. I could never say anything back to defend myself as it just made matters even worse.

I accepted all the screaming and the shouting and the words. They were only words. I just let them go in one ear and out the other. Ignore them and everything would be alright.

One day I wrote a letter to my nan after mum had had a go at me, pleading with her to let me come back to live with them as I was lonely, and I'd had enough of my mum's rantings. It was one of those letters you write but never intend to send because I knew it would break my mum's heart. If I had left her, she would see me as choosing my dad over her. She would never forgive me, and I didn't want to see her unhappy or hurt her feelings.

I had mentioned it once in passing during a conversation with my nan over the phone, about the possibility of maybe coming back. Still, I was never really serious about it, but my nan said it was impossible. She was now a little bit older, seventy-eight years old, and wouldn't be able to cope with me and my dad, especially now I was a teenager and would be 'getting up to things teenagers get up to.' More importantly, neither she nor my dad could afford to keep me, not on my nan's pension and his wages. It was out of the question. My letter was a begging letter saying how much I missed her and dad. I would do anything to help out, I would buy my own alarm clock, so I could get up early and do a paper round to support myself, and then I'd get a Saturday job and pay my way. She wouldn't have to spend much. I wouldn't eat much, and I would be on my best behaviour. I'd help her with all the housework and cooking. Therefore, I'd actually be a benefit and help to have around. I could look after her in her old age. It was a letter you never intend to send; I was going to tear it up and throw it away. I left the letter hidden in my bedroom, in my desk and went to school. It was a Monday, so mum was at home.

When I returned from school at lunchtime, I found my mum sat on the sofa with the neighbour from upstairs. It had been a great morning, and I walked in with a spring in my step. "Hi, Mum. Hi, Sonia." The smile on my face slowly disappeared. I could see from my mum's facial expression she wasn't having the same morning I was. Her face was full of sadness as if her world had been taken from her. "Mum, what's the matter? What's wrong?" I couldn't understand what the problem could be. I sat down beside her, concerned. "Mum. Talk to me! What is it?" My mum held up a piece of paper. I didn't know what it was at first and then it slowly dawned on me. Very slowly, everything went cold and came to a standstill. I couldn't believe it. She had been in my room, found my letter and read it.

She had been sneaking around my bedroom.

"Is this how you feel?" she asked, holding up the letter.

"Mum, no. I can explain, it's nothing. It's just writing. It's nothing. I didn't mean it, please."

"You wrote this. Is this how much you want to go back to live with your dad?" She started to cry. "You want to go back to England and leave me?"

"No. No, of course I don't. I want to stay here with you." The neighbour just sat there, watching in silence.

"I have already spoken to your nan, and she says you can go back and live with them. I just want you to be happy, so if you're going to be happy there then go and live with your dad. Your flight is already booked. Sonia, would you like another cup of coffee?"

Chapter 9

The Business

*The body, however, is not meant for sexual immorality but
for the Lord, and the Lord for the body.*
- 1 Corinthians 6:13 NIV

Some of the people who turned up at my mum's place just came to see her and stop and have a chat as they were passing through the area. A lot of the men looked upon her as a mother figure, and she looked on them as the sons she never had.

It was nice to see the regulars, it may have been months since we last saw them, so it was like seeing old friends. The atmosphere was so natural but at the same time surreal, but that's how it was in Spain and unfortunately still is today. Whether people are aware of it and prepared to accept it or not, it is what it is – the world's oldest profession. My mum owned a massage parlour for over sixteen years. Although prostitution in Spain is not legal, it isn't illegal either, it's tolerated. Pimping is illegal, so is soliciting on the streets which can be dangerous.

Over the years she had built up a large clientele. There were genuinely nice guys, good looking men, and some not so good looking. Young, old, fat, thin, tall and short. Chefs from the local restaurants, judges, barristers, along with famous racing car drivers and a few other famous people whose names shall always remain a secret.

There may be some people reading this now who might think this an unsavoury topic and have some moral qualms which I respect and understand; but having lived it and been part of it regardless of the moral issues, this is my story. I am not defending myself for the situation my mum's business put me in, as it was out of my control. Only God can judge us. But, years down the line - transformed, redeemed, and seeing things through God's eyes, I can say this; looking back, I see a world of corruption, full of darkness, no matter how you want to dress it up. It doesn't matter how pretty the girls looked, or how beautiful, plush, and comfortable the furnishings and decorations were, it was all wrong. Temptation and sin – all cleverly disguised. How sad am I now? I can't go back to fix any of it. I can't go back and tell those women and men how mistaken we all were and try to help those women in other ways. What does the alternative look like? I did not know what the alternative was in those days. In trying to do right, what my mum was doing was wrong. Deep in her heart, she knew it was wrong, she didn't really want me to be a part of any of it, not her own daughter, nor for anybody else's daughter.

The business was a part of my life from the age of sixteen. I say "a part of it" as I didn't always live in Spain. I was always flitting backwards and forwards until I met Liam. A man I believe was sent from God, to become my rock, my anchor and protector.

Mum sold the only thing she had left, which was the apartment she bought with the money from the sale of our house in London.

She had no money, no savings, no job, and with me living in England, no daughter to look after. With the money from the sale of the flat, she rented a cheap apartment in a 'not so desirable' area, fifteen minutes outside Barcelona, and the rest she used to rent a larger flat, one just outside the city centre. This larger apartment she used as a "Massage Parlour", which is a nicer way of referring to a brothel. The flat itself wasn't the best, but it served its purpose. As long as it was kept clean and the service was good, the men would return. There were four bedrooms, two bathrooms, a good-sized lounge, small kitchen, and a large, dark, covered patio which was ideal for drying all the towels and bed linen.

In the early days of starting up the business, mum had to do all the washing and drying herself. The poor old washing machine and tumble dryer were in constant use. The flat itself went round in a circle. You could walk from the lounge into the hallway, past the bedrooms and bathrooms and straight back into the lounge. It was a great way to hide clients who did not want to bump into other clients while walking along the corridor. It was also useful for making quick getaways by going around the back of the flat without being seen by men waiting for their turn in the lounge; ideal for when girls arrived late for work. The lounge was the only room to receive natural light as it was the only part of the flat to face the exterior, looking out onto a busy main road.

The rest of the flat was dark and in my opinion a bit eerie. I felt uncomfortable walking along the corridor. I would switch on all the lights to get from one end of the flat to the other. The carpets were worn in places, and they seemed to have a damp, sticky feel about them underfoot. As you walked in the front door, you were led from the entrance hall into the lounge where the men would be seated and informed about the different girls on duty and the types of services available. In the left-hand corner was a small bar area, with a couple of stools, from where mum would serve drinks while the men casually chatted amongst themselves - as if they had known each other for years - about the latest football results or other topics, whilst they waited for the girls to be available from a previous service. A close eye would be kept on the levels of alcohol in the bottles that were consumed, ensuring it was only the clients drinking from them and not the girls necking back a quick one while no one was looking. They all knew drinking while on duty was forbidden unless it had been bought for them by a client, and then it was supposed to be a soft drink. Some of the men liked to buy their chosen girl a drink so they could sit and chit-chat before getting down to more serious business. In the middle of the room, under the window, was a sofa and in front of that, a desk used for the administration side of things. To the right of the sofa was an archway which was partitioned off by drab brown curtains, which hid a small section of the room where the girls sat. This was known as the 'girls' room. It was tiny. Here they prepared themselves and touched up their make-up before heading out to make their introductions.

Crammed into this space was a three-seater sofa with two armchairs either side, facing each other. There was a small coffee table, usually with the odd empty glass of Coca Cola, an ashtray overflowing with cigarette butts, ash and splatters of spilt coffee covering whatever little bit of table was left. A small television tucked away in the corner on mute showing one of the soaps, until all the men had left the room. Then the volume could be turned back up, and the curtain opened once again. With the curtains closed there was just enough room for the girls to take off their rabbit character slippers and replace them with their stilettos. Most of the furniture was second-hand from the local flea market, which is not a market that has fleas but does have cheap second-hand and brand-new furniture. (If you wanted second-hand stuff with fleas, I'm sure you would easily come across it.) It is a tremendous market, a must-see for those who visit Barcelona, *Los Encantes,* as it is commonly known.

Mum placed adverts in the local daily newspapers regularly. Two different adverts to be exact. One in the "jobs offered" section stating, "Girls wanted for Sauna of Relax" and a second one advertising the sauna itself, between the many other establishments being advertised. The adverts were costly but essential to the business. She negotiated good rates, and the salesman advised her on what to say in comparison to the others. Most important of all at the bottom of the advert it would say, "We Speak English". She wanted to attract as many people as possible: if you could draw the English-speaking tourists as well, then that was a bonus - especially when the International Business Conference was taking place. The advertising guy managed her account for the next sixteen years and became a good friend.

In the beginning, days would go by where mum would be on her own with no girls or clients. Some days she would be on her own with just one or two girls and then no clients. Soon she found herself with the odd client and no girls. She would offer the men free drinks and tell them to come back another day when she had recruited more girls. The men would sit with my mum and talk for ages, wanting to know how a woman of her age had ended up running a place like this with no experience, no man to protect her, totally on her own, trying to run a sauna. What was she thinking? It is a dangerous job for a single woman. Was she crazy? But it wasn't too long before the girls and clients started to coincide, and the business began to take shape. Mum hardly ever went back to the apartment. She lived, worked, and slept twenty-four-seven at the sauna. She couldn't leave the building as she didn't have a receptionist. She had to be there to answer the phone, answer the door and do the cleaning and serve the drinks.

It was some time before I found out about mum's business as I was only sixteen; I had no idea as I was back in England. She was very apprehensive of what I would think of her and what my reaction would be. She wanted to protect me, she knew I was underage and therefore, she didn't want me to know about these sorts of things. I booked a flight to visit my mum, one of my many trips to keep her company when she was feeling down and lonely. I was always on the lookout for cheap flights. Any last-minute flight would do, as long as it was under a hundred pounds. Those were the days before the low budget airlines, with their unbelievably cheap flights, sometimes for a penny if you were lucky. One day as we spoke on the phone, my mum felt the need to tell me what she had been up to for the past few months. I wondered if she would be working during my stay and how much time we would get to spend together. With apprehension, she told me of her new business venture. She commented on how nice the clients were and how they had supported her when she didn't have any girls. Now the business was starting to take shape. She was slowly getting more and more clients and lots of different types of girls who were all lovely young ladies, out of work and looking for a way to make some money. She felt sad for some of them as they made her think of me; some of these girls were so young, they could have been her daughters. I wasn't far from turning eighteen myself, just another year or so. She explained how some of the girls were at university studying degrees – one of them was studying to be a doctor. They were on the game so they could pay for their university fees. I was slightly taken aback at her news if I am honest, and I was ashamed of her for a while, my own mum. And now I'm ashamed of feeling ashamed. How judgemental of me? As mum pointed out in her very sure way of pointing things out, I should be proud of her, all the hard work she was putting into the business to make things work, all on her own. Having to give up her daughter because she could no longer

116

afford to feed her, sending her back to live with her father. After all those years of being on her own and struggling to make ends meet, now I was a teenager I should be looking after her, not leaving her when she needed me most.

"You don't want to see me on the streets do you, begging for money?" She would ask. "This is how I can finally make some money. For the first time in my life, I have my own money, and I can buy myself some new clothes. I don't care what people think. All I care about is my daughter and myself. No one ever looked after me. No one ever looked after us, did they? Your father never gave me a penny to look after you." This was the same sermon I would get as her defence when having to justify herself. "When I was brought up by the nuns, I had nothing you know, nothing!"

I could see her point. "When I was working in the other sauna as a cleaner, I saw how they were robbing the clients and the girls. They even had underage girls working there. They were a bunch of crooks, you know. Here I have girls over the age of eighteen. I ask for their ID and their papers. I make sure they are not doing drugs and they are all clean. Otherwise, they are not allowed to work here. The police know I am here. One of the local police officers came to visit to see what I was doing here while he was doing his rounds. I told him my daughter has had to go back to England and live with her father, and I am here on my own struggling."

So, I was happy for her, she was happy, and yes, she was finally earning some money. She was earning more money than she had ever earned before. "The policeman was nice and told me I must be crazy to be doing this, a woman on my own with no protection. He was kind so I gave him a drink. He told me if I had any problems to call him at the station. I told him if I come across any stolen credit cards,

I refuse them, and I call the police." That was one of the reasons mum's sauna was successful, because of her honesty and always keeping on the right side of the law. She always abided by the rules, and all her clients knew it. They always returned, even if it was just for a chat to see how she was and have a drink or to go with one of the women. None of the women there were being exploited or controlled by a pimp. They were there of their own free-will and volition, in order to put food on the table. If any of them did have a pimp controlling them, my mum refused to have anything to do with them. That side of things was a completely different ball game. She was offering women a safe place where they weren't going to get ripped off and no harm was going to come to them. The policeman's name was Pedro, and I felt reassured knowing he was looking out for her. She had made a new friend who she could call if she were in any trouble. Pedro became a good friend to her over the years and always gave her good advice. We often went out for meals together with his wife and his two teenage children. When Christmas came, she would buy them lavish presents as a show of her gratitude for Pedro's support. Little did I know what this friendship was going to cost years down the line.

Once having come through security and passport control, I retrieved my suitcase from the baggage reclaim and jumped into the next taxi – from the long line of black and yellow taxis, patiently waiting their turn sometimes for up to two hours, in the hope of a good fare and told the driver my destination. Most of the time, mum didn't come to the airport to collect me. Usually, she would be waiting for me at home or busy at work. After a drive across town, I arrived at the sauna. Mum was waiting for me outside, ready to pay the taxi driver. We went for a quick coffee in the bar next door. She was excited and happy to see me as always but also nervous, as was I. I was going to see my mother's sauna for the first time, and she was anxious about my reaction. We checked the streets to make sure no one was looking or spying on us as I, an underaged young girl, entered the sauna. We laughed nervously as we ran up the stairs to the first floor. She opened the door, and we walked in. I felt excited as this was a whole new adventure for mum, and it felt like we were going places. Mum's life was finally on the up.

There were three girls in the flat waiting for clients to turn up, hoping to be chosen. The atmosphere was very relaxed, the television was on, and the girls were lounging on the sofa. One was reading a book while another one filed her nails. I was introduced to these young women, lovely-looking women only a few years older than me. They were ordinary people; they didn't have two heads or walked differently to me. They were there to earn money to pay the bills, pay their rent and feed their children. They were so happy to meet me. It was as if they already knew me after hearing mum's life story. They could spend a lot of hours waiting for clients to show up while working in a sauna and they got to listen to a lot of stories about people and their lives.

Mum proudly showed me around the flat, then the doorbell rang. Quickly I ran and hid behind the curtain in the girls' room. I sat with my legs up on an old leather armchair next to the three girls I had just met. They were busy strutting around in skimpy outfits along with feet crippling high heels. My heart was beating with excitement. We all giggled nervously like naughty schoolgirls who knew they were doing wrong, with an element of excitement at the thought of being caught. If I had been caught then we would have been in big trouble. I had just turned seventeen. I had another year to go before it was legal for me to be on the premises. A man came in and sat down on the sofa while mum sat next to him and informed him of the various services the girls had to offer. As he considered all this, the girls took turns in coming out from behind the curtain and introduced themselves. As they left the tiny, partitioned room, they each checked themselves in the mirror, fiddled with their hair a bit and put on a fresh coating of lipstick. I sat as far back as I could in the armchair so as not to be seen, holding my breath. One by one, they went through. I could hear them kissing their 'hellos' on each cheek and introducing themselves. "*Hola*, my name is Lola." Lola would then turn and head back behind the curtain; then it was the next girl's turn, and so on. I heard mum talking to the man, and a couple of minutes later she stuck her head through the curtain and called Lola. Lola grabbed her toiletry bag, a couple of condoms and headed off to one of the bedrooms where the client was already waiting for her.

Mum was too nervous to let me stay any longer, so she told me to go back downstairs to the bar and wait for her there and we would then go to get some lunch.

On Sundays, the sauna was closed, and mum was too tired to go all the way to the other side of town to the empty flat which barely had any furniture in, so she stayed in the sauna and slept there. It was a flat after all. I was able to stay with her then, as she could say it was her home, which technically it was. I wasn't too happy staying there when it was empty with no one around. The business was going well, and word was getting around; "A lovely woman on her own has opened a new sauna where you can go with your mates on your way home after a good night out." Clients were coming back time after time and bringing their friends. They were always welcomed and made to feel very comfortable. The girls were also thrilled as they were earning good money, more money than in some of the other houses. Word spread around the girls too, and there were lots of girls phoning up wanting to come and work at mums. The girls were paid on a fifty-fifty basis, not like some other saunas where they were paid a forty-sixty split and sometimes didn't get paid at all. In some places the clients would pay for a high-end service, but the receptionist would tell the girl it was for a cheaper one, stealing the difference from the girl. Here, the girls were told how much the service was going to be as she went to the room. The client paid the girl direct, and then she would come out and hand the money to the receptionist. That way everyone knew precisely what was being paid for and the girls would keep a tally of the services they had provided during the night and everyone was happy.

Mum was very picky about the type of girls she took on. No one under eighteen, proof of ID would be asked for and photocopied, no drugs or anything undesirable. They all had regular check-ups with a recommended gynaecologist. There were girls whose families or husbands thought they were working in an office. Others believed they were off to their cleaning jobs. Little did they know what they were really doing. The husband may have been out of work with no money coming in, and with two or three children to feed, plus no income support from the Spanish system, thus the wife took it upon herself to provide for the family as best she could. That was a huge sacrifice for any woman to make. In those days, once you were married, you were expected to become a housewife for the rest of your life and bring up the children. It was frowned upon for a woman to be out working and extremely hard to get a job in the first place. One of the girls had been kicked out of her rented apartment because she could not pay the rent, so she did double shifts and just stayed and slept at the sauna during the week apart from Sundays when it was closed.

She would sleep in one of the rooms when it wasn't busy or remain asleep during the day shift, ready to work the night shift. The day shift was always much quieter than the night shift. She was temporarily homeless, so mum allowed her to stay. Once she had saved some money, she could find somewhere new to rent. It wasn't long before mum needed a bigger place.

While I was back in England and studying at college, mum would keep me informed of how things were progressing and stories about the interesting people who came to visit. I always looked forward to my next visit.

I returned a couple of months later for a long weekend. This time mum did come and collect me from the airport and took me to her new flat which she had recently bought. She had given notice on the rented flat and purchased a lovely new one in a sought-after area in the south of Barcelona. It had a beautiful private park area for residents of the estate with swings and slides and a bowls area where the older generation could sit or watch others playing.

The flat was lovely, although compact, as many apartments are in Barcelona. However, it had four bedrooms and two bathrooms. It was high up giving us fantastic views over to Montjuic and the Olympic stadium. It really was incredible. Mum had been busy buying all the furniture from the local department store.

Lovely flat, beautiful furniture and nice clothes; for the first-time mum was living how she always dreamed, not scrimping and scraping. No longer was she selling tobacco in the middle of the night. After I had settled in and dumped my bags in what was my own new bedroom we went downstairs and had a coffee at the local bar. She loved going to the local bar where you could have a three-course meal for just 600 pesetas and chat with the owner, Isabel. She was a charming lady and thought very highly of mum. We then jumped in a taxi and mum took me to see the new sauna she had set up in the centre of the city. It was a stunning old building with beautiful high ceilings. It was lovely.

It was a huge five-bedroom apartment with a long hallway and a large reception room at each end where the clients used to wait their turn. Both reception rooms had big, comfy sofas and a television. The five large bedrooms ran along the hallway, and each was referred to by its colour - the white room, the blue room, yellow, pink, and green. Every room had its own washing facilities and toilet; three of them had bidets and sinks. The two largest rooms had big round sunken baths. It's funny how everyone had their favourite room. Even mum and I, when we were tired, would choose a specific room to go and sleep in. Partway along the corridor was a section partitioned off where the girls sat and watched their own TV and waited for a client to come along. Again, like in the original flat, they would hide behind the curtain when people arrived. They had a small coffee table to put all their bits on and a tiny TV in the corner which was always on and only really watched when it wasn't too busy. We were forever telling them to turn the volume down. When there were no men about, the curtain would be open and the girls were able to go and sit in the reception areas and watch the bigger television, or they would sit and do some knitting or play Scrabble. Anything to while the hours away. As usual for Spanish nightlife, it never started to get busy until around two in the morning onwards. This was when all the crowds appeared after they had finished their meals and were ready to party before heading home to their wives and girlfriends, and yes, most of them, I am sad to say, did have girlfriends and wives.

Thursday, Friday, and Saturday nights were the busiest nights of the week when all the young guys came out to play. Both receptions would be full of men talking to each other about the last Barcelona football match, how they were getting on at work or the latest new car which had just been advertised. Men greeted each other as friends. They would comment on how long it had been since they last saw one another and how come they have not been lately. Some of them knew each other from years of coming to the sauna and would then leave together and go on to a recommended bar which had recently opened, "Here, take my card, tell them Juan sent you."

As soon as I turned eighteen, my mum wanted me to help her at work, and I became a supervisor. We always said supervisor, although receptionist does sound much nicer. "This is my business Evie, and if it's my business then it is your business too, and you need to learn how to run it. I don't want to run it for too much longer, not at my age." Was my mum seriously expecting me to take over what now seemed to be 'the family firm'? Oh my gosh, I thought, I can't do this, I'm not able to deal with this. Running a massage parlour when I grew up was never on my agenda. I was against the whole thing. It was wrong, the entire thing was wrong, but it seemed I didn't have any say or choice in the matter. In a sense, it had nothing to do with me, I was just there living my life with my mum. It had been her only option, this or starve and not be able to provide for your child, along with all these other women who also had no other alternative. For the last couple of years, I had dreamed of running my own travel company, sending people away on fantastic and exciting holidays to exotic faraway places - not run a massage parlour.

Mum was doing well, so was the business. The girls were going home every morning with a purse full of notes and incredibly happy. Mum had employed a supervisor and my job when I was visiting her for short holidays was to supervise the supervisor, allowing mum to have a rest at home or go and have a meal in the local bingo hall. There was a waiter who doubled up as a doorman for my mum, and his purpose was to show some presence. As soon as there was ever any sign of trouble, mum would start waving her arms, screaming, and threatening to call the police in true Spanish dramatic fashion. "I have friends in very high places you know, and all I have to do is pick up the phone and the police will be here before I put the phone down." People never knew if she was lying or not, but she was very convincing, and it was true. She only had to make one call to Pedro, and there would be a whole squad team at the front door in minutes. They were quite surprised at this small middle-aged woman running this sort of business and how brave she was to take on anyone who dared to confront her. They would normally retract and walk away peacefully, concerned at how crazy this woman seemed to be.

Once a guy came into the sauna who, strangely enough, knew the entire layout of the building and, conveniently, the time at which the girls were paid. He had never been before as we always remembered a face. He came in, and as he was shown to the reception area, he opened the curtain to the girls' room and grabbed hold of one of the girls. He took her by the arm and held a knife to her throat. He then shuffled her back along the hallway to the office where mum was cashing up and paying the girls. Mum just sat barely lifting her eyes from the money in front of her. "Give me all the money, or I'll cut this girl's throat." He said.

She just sat there, staring at him.

"Give me the money, or I'll cut her throat."

"Go on then," still unphased.

"I'll cut her throat."

"Go on then, she has nothing to do with me, but you are not getting a single peseta of this money." Mum knew this had to be a setup, an inside job.

"You can do what you want to her, she doesn't belong to me." The man stood there in disbelief. Mum stood up slowly and grabbed hold of the chair next to her and threw it at him. As it flew towards him, he let go of the girl, cutting himself in the process. He turned around and fled along with the girl close behind. Mum was obviously shaken, but he didn't get a single peseta of the girls' or my mum's share of the money. She then proceeded to call the police who came round very shortly after to check she was alright and take down descriptions of the man and woman. I think my mum was extremely brave to act as she did and stand up to him in that way. I would have just given him the money and prayed he left without hurting anyone. That night the waiter got the sack for not helping or attempting to tackle the man. Word of mum's courage and bravery travelled fast.

There were two shifts, a day shift and a night shift. The day shift started at eleven in the morning until nine at night. Then the night shift started at nine until seven in the morning. The cleaner arrived at seven every morning and would start cleaning the rooms and the rest of the sauna from top to bottom, ready for the following shift. During the day, the clientele was much older. There was a marked difference in the number of clients who visited during the day compared to those who came at night. The days were quiet and with not much activity. Thank goodness for daytime TV! At approximately 8.30 p.m. the girls for the night shift would start drifting in. The whole atmosphere changed. "Evening, how are you?" They would catch up on what they had been getting up to during the day, the shops they had visited and would parade the wares they had bought. Showers start to run; hairdryers begin to blow, and the place starts to come alive again.

"Have you seen my lipstick anywhere?"

"Can I borrow your hairdryer?"

The phone begins to ring with clients asking for information and directions. What time are you open until? How many girls do you have? Do you do visits to hotels? Not forgetting the heavy breathers down the phone and the kids making prank phone calls.

Still, it kept us busy, getting up and down answering the phone and opening the door.

Nine o'clock arrives. "Right, who is missing? Where is Sofia tonight? Is she coming? Have you heard from Rebecca?"

The doorbell rings every few minutes with the girls from the night shift arriving and the day shift girls going home. *"Hasta mañana,"* they yell as they leave, closing the door behind them.

9.30 p.m. the doorbell rings. "You're late, you know you are supposed to be here for 8.30, what if I had a room full of clients waiting?" says the supervisor testily. In one ear and out the other as far as the girls are concerned. "I won't let you in tomorrow if you arrive late," threatens the supervisor. They know this is a bluff.

The first job you do as a supervisor when you arrive, like any other business, is to manage the changeover. Check the day's takings and that all the rooms are clean and presentable, and all the bins have been cleaned and are spotless. Check there is enough ice in the ice machine, the bar area is fully stocked, and all the glasses are clean and ready for a busy night ahead. Believe me, when you spend all night opening and shutting doors, answering telephones; loading and unloading the washing machine and tumble dryer, you don't get a moment to sit down and relax. You had to make sure everything was ready and prepared. Once everything has been checked then the girls start placing their orders for dinner.

"Right, tonight I think I fancy Chinese."

"I want pizza."

"*Calamares a la Romana* for me please, and a packet of Fortuna cigarettes."

"Yes, one at a time please." The supervisor phones the local restaurants and orders the various meal requests for the girls and for herself, then she phones the local taxi company and asks them to go and collect it all. It was a great system.

"Come on, come on, hurry up, what if a client turns up now and sees you all half-dressed with no make-up on? Go and get ready and make yourselves look beautiful," encourages the supervisor. The doorbell rings and the first clients of the evening start arriving. Sometimes they preferred to wait until all the girls are ready, happy to sit with a free drink in their hand watching the evening news.

I remember there was a girl whose client had complained about her, saying she wasn't very good and was acting a bit funny. I was on my own supervising as mum had decided to stay at home. The other girls had complained about her as well, but I wasn't quite sure how to approach the situation without having any proof of anything untoward. Everyone thought she was on drugs, hence her funny behaviour and being a bit off with the others. "Okay, I will sort it out, leave it to me." I said. I had to do something, but what? I couldn't just go up to her and accuse her of being rude and send her home. I kept an eye on her, watching her every move. She kept going to the toilet which I thought was a bit suspicious. "Are you alright in there?" I asked as I stood outside the toilet door.

"Yes, I'm fine, thank you."

"Can you come out now, please, I need to talk to you."

"Yes, hold on." A couple of minutes passed, and still nothing.

"Come out now please," Still no movement. I bent down and looked through the keyhole. There was a silence down the corridor, and the rest of the girls were peering around the curtain of their room, holding their breath, surprised at my tone of authority. Through the keyhole, to my horror, I could see the girl on her knees sniffing lines of cocaine off the toilet seat - something I had only seen in films. Knowing how mum disapproved of drugs in the workplace, I immediately started to bang on the door.

"Open this door right now!" I commanded.

"What's wrong?" came the voice from the other side of the door.

"Open this door right now and come out before I break it down." What was I saying, and how was I saying it? I frightened myself. The girls looked on in amazement.

Slowly the door opened, and she walked back to the girls' area. "What's the matter?" she asked as if nothing was going on.

"I want you to get your things and leave right now."

"Why? What have I done?" still playing the innocent.

"Do you want me to ask you to empty your bag and show me what you have in there? Please get your things and leave. If you don't, I will call the police. We don't tolerate that sort of behaviour in this house." The girl packed up her bits and left quietly. I went and sat down at the other end of the corridor. There was silence in the house for a while after. I sat there shaking and scared, I had never done anything like that before, but I had dealt with it. Where had that strength and

129

boldness come from to deal with that situation? The girls were relieved and carried on with the rest of their evening.

Mum loved it when I came to visit. She was so proud to have her daughter with her, knowing she could sit back and relax while I was there. Instead of going to work herself, she would send me in her place. She knew while I was there no one would try and steal money from the till or pull any fast ones.

There were a couple of awkward times when a client wasn't happy with his service - I found this incredibly unnerving. I should say the client hadn't completed his task and his time was up; and when your time is up, your time is up. If you needed more time, then you had to pay again, those were the rules. Occasionally, some men may have had a bit too much to drink, not the girl's fault, and they wanted more time. I really didn't like dealing with this sort of scenario, but I had to take care of it. It didn't happen very often, but on this occasion, I was the one who was called into the room, with the girl and the client.

The air was thick and warm, it felt oppressive. The man was frustrated, angry and completely naked. Okay, this is fine, you can do this, I said to myself. It's not every day you have a totally naked man standing in front of you shouting at you. He was the same height as me, as I remember trying to keep eye contact with him. He was hot and sweaty and trying to intimidate me with his nakedness. He explained his discontent and blamed the girl for his lack of performance and kept encroaching on my space. Just keep eye contact, I thought to myself. Forget the fact he is naked, just don't give in. I am in charge and if he wants more time, he is going to have to pay for another service. I explained the rules to the man very calmly and empathised with him, and the girl had been in the room long enough. If he needed more time, it wasn't going to be for free. All he had to do was calm down, and I'd get him a drink, maybe a Coca Cola, this time on the house. By this point, he was pretty much in my face, I didn't lose eye contact, and I didn't falter. He relented and agreed to pay for another half an hour but with a different girl. This suited us all, as the original girl had had enough of him. A new girl came in, she was happy, he was pleased, and I was relieved that the problem had been resolved peacefully.

I, myself was really taken aback at how I had stood up to this man without wavering. How had I managed it?

****

After mum died, I abandoned the business, literally. I shudder to think what my life might have looked like if I had kept it going. It wasn't even an option. The thought of it makes me sick. It had nothing to do with me, it was all my mum's. I think you could say we had been living in fantasyland, blinkered, hypnotised by temptation with all its falseness and the illusions that go with it. Sometimes we refuse to see the wrong we are doing because the truth is too hard to stomach. It wasn't long before I told the girls to all go home and closed the premises, I never once looked back or wanted to. It was as if it never existed, wiped clean from the slate. But, for my mother at the time and likewise for so many other women, it seemed to be the only option to survive. Then it seemed exciting, everything was new. It offered so much promise, money, materialistic things, food and security. It is so sad that women felt they had to do that - and they still do, to this day, not just in Spain but around the world.

Unfortunately, back then it seemed natural because my mum, society, the men, and the women made it the norm. Television

131

programmes and the films on TV of an adult nature which were, and still are shown, make it acceptable. If we talk about certain topics often enough, we begin to normalise them, until they become second nature to us. Eventually they become tolerated by the law, even though they may be morally wrong. Being constantly exposed to it, it becomes a natural way of thinking. But to many people on the outside looking in, these things can seem tragic, wrong, shameful. So many women who work as prostitutes - voluntarily or not - are believed to end up suffering from mental health issues or nervous breakdowns and can feel riddled with guilt and shame. God did not create us to be riddled with guilt and shame, that's why He sent His one and only son into this world, Jesus, so we can be free from guilt, shame and lies. That is why He died on the cross, for you and me. So, we no longer have to believe the lies. The lies that we tell ourselves; that we aren't good enough, we will never succeed at anything, we're not pretty or handsome enough. We have been given a way out from temptation and sin.

Some people say there's always another option, we make our own choices. The men who were visiting the sauna were looking for one thing, sex. You could compare it to, stories in the Old Testament in the Bible, about orgies, human sacrifices made to false gods, whom the people idolised and worshipped - imaginary idols.

How much pain, hurt, deceit, and lies were being created in my mum's place and thousands of others like it?

Once everybody had gone home, the place was empty and strangely quiet, you could sense a different energy. A thick heavy presence, an energy sitting quietly, waiting in the corner.

It wasn't a comfortable feeling being around all the drinking of alcohol, pornography and possibly the drugs that had been taken before entering or after leaving the place. There's nothing glamorous about the business. Where does all that come from? Who tempts us? Who presents it to us? It's not just Spain where all these things happen. It's happening all around the world; people, make the wrong choices. Perhaps turn to drink, drugs, pornography and may become addicted.

People don't want to be told how to live their life and don't want to be told what is sinful. The more we turn away from God, the less aware we are of sin and temptation in our lives. Forgetting He's there to protect us. He is the Father who guides us, and we need Him so desperately. Like any good, loving, caring, parent He gives us boundaries, and they are there for a reason. We have rules and boundaries in football, rugby, golf - any and every sport. We are happy to obey them - and we get upset when someone doesn't play by those rules, but some of us refuse to live by His guidelines. We have rules at work, they are there for a purpose, to keep us safe. What is it that's so good at tempting us? What is the purpose behind it? Is it to separate us further from God?

Yes, the men were friendly enough. They were ordinary people, just like you, reading this book right now. What was the one thing on their mind? To satisfy themselves. I don't agree with all that happened then, I don't condone it in any shape or form. I wouldn't want any woman to be in that situation, having to work by selling her body; I regard it as the selling of souls, souls that should belong to God.

Chapter 10

Just A Few Questions

"Have I not commanded you? Be strong and courageous.
Do not be afraid; do not be discouraged,
for the Lord your God will be with you wherever you go."
- Joshua 1:9 NIV

It was early evening, a Tuesday, I think. The actual day of the week isn't really of much importance it is the sequence of events that matter. I was at home in England with my then boyfriend, Simon. We had just finished dinner and I thought I would give my mum a ring at work. I wanted to say hello and see how things were going and what she had been up to since I last spoke to her three days ago. For some reason she wasn't there, so I ended up talking to the supervisor.

"Where's Mum?" I enquired, thinking it was unusual for her not to be there at that time in the evening. She was usually getting ready to do the changeover of shifts.

"Oh, Evie. The police were here earlier, saying we had underage girls and of course we don't. You know how strict your mum is about that sort of thing. Anyway, she offered to go down to the police station to help them with their enquiries. Apparently, they have found underage girls working in other saunas in the city, she wanted to help the police but should be back soon."

"Oh, my word, that's dreadful, how could they think such a thing? Mum would never do that she always checks their papers."

"They searched the place and questioned all the girls, but they didn't find anyone, so they can't say anything or do anything."

"Okay, tell her to phone me when she gets back. Are you guys all okay?"

"Yeah, yeah, we are fine, just getting ready for the night shift. Why don't you phone you know who and see if he can give you any information about what is going on, he's bound to know something."

"Yes, good idea, I'll give him a call now." I put the phone down, feeling not quite right. Something was wrong. I had a funny feeling about this. It was all a bit bizarre. I picked up the phone to call him, he would know what was going on.

"Hola, I hope I am not disturbing you," I said, not really giving a damn if I was.

"No, you're fine," he replied.

"I just phoned work, and they told me what has happened. The police have taken mum to the station, why?" I was starting to sound a bit anxious.

"Yes, she is fine, she is just helping us out with some information. There has been a raid on all the saunas in the area. Don't worry. Some saunas had underage girls. She'll be back soon."

"But they didn't find any girls though, did they?"

"No, of course not. You know your mum, Evie, she's not stupid. Listen, stop worrying, it is just standard procedure. She'll be fine."

I put the phone down. Why did I not believe him? He was very cool and calm. Of course, he knew about the raid, he may have helped organise it. It was the first time anything major like this had happened. It all seemed very weird.

I ran downstairs to tell Simon what had happened, and he just stared at me blankly. "Well, there is nothing you can do at the minute. Give her a ring later and see what happened." I sat down to watch the television, but I felt twitchy. I couldn't relax knowing mum was being questioned by the police when she needn't be, and especially when there was no evidence of anything untoward. I gave it a couple of hours before I rang work again, giving her plenty of time to get back and make a cup of coffee. It was now ten o'clock at night.

"Well?" I asked the supervisor, "any news, is she back yet?"

"No, nothing."

"Right, I'll give him another call and see what is going on."

"Hi, only me. There is still no word from my mum, do you know if she has left the station yet?"

"It's okay, they are keeping her in overnight. She is fine and she should be out tomorrow morning."

"I beg your pardon! What do you mean they are keeping her in overnight? She hasn't done anything. There was no evidence of any girls being underage, you said so yourself."

I was starting to get angry. They had no right to do this; this was my mum we were talking about. My mum doesn't go to prison. What the hell was going on?

She has never been in trouble with the law, she was in her fifties, and she hadn't done anything wrong.

"She'll be out tomorrow morning, call her then." He was so calm and relaxed, but it wasn't his mother in prison, well not technically prison, but in a cell overnight. I didn't care where it was. There was an injustice going on here, and no one was doing anything about it.

I called work again to tell them what was happening, and they were horrified, but it was business as usual at the sauna. I told the supervisor I would give her an update in the morning. All I could do was wait.

I hardly slept at all that night. I kept wondering how mum was doing, what she would be up to, and how she was feeling. Apparently, they had taken mum's cousin, Susi as well. She had gone along with mum to keep her company. Mum had taken Susi on as a daytime supervisor as she and her family had fallen on hard times, and her husband's business had gone bust. They were desperate.

The next morning the first thing I did was call the sauna, no news there, then I called Pedro again.

"Well?"

"Yeah, everything is good. They are going to keep her in for a few days. She'll be fine, no need to worry."

"The hell they are, I'm coming over straightaway."

"There's nothing you can do. You're wasting your time; she'll be out in three to four days."

Before he had time to finish his sentence, I had put the phone down and had grabbed my bag and passport. I had a plane to catch, and I wasn't going to miss it. I ran downstairs shouting at Simon.

"They're keeping her in for a few days he says. They have no evidence, and they're keeping her in! On what grounds? They can't do that! What about her tablets?" I was furious. She had no one to help her, no one to bail her out but me.

"I have to go and sort this out and get her out of prison. Are you coming with me?"

"Yes, of course I am." Simon was working on a window cleaning round with a friend, who was hoping Simon would take over his business once he had retired. He was able to up and go - the good thing about being self-employed, I guess.

We caught the first plane out from Luton heading to Barcelona. After landing we jumped in a taxi and headed straight for the police station where mum was being held, along with a group of girls from various saunas from the area. Mum wasn't where I thought she was going to be. I had to make numerous phone calls to various police stations insisting someone give me information. I wanted them to tell me where and why she was being held, and when she would be released. We eventually found out she was being moved to another central police station near *Las Ramblas*. All I could do was go and wait outside and hope I could see her when they arrived. Simon and I waited in the street outside the station all afternoon and into the early evening. We didn't have any keys to the flat, my mum had those, I hoped she would be allowed to give them to me.

Finally, a police van pulled up and a group of women were escorted out of the van and ushered into the police station. I was beside myself by this point, I had been crying in disbelief most of the afternoon. It all seemed like a bad dream. I caught a glimpse of my mum and asked her if she was alright.

Mum gave a massive sigh of relief and cried out, "Oh, *mi hija!*" (Oh, my daughter.) She was so happy to see me and became relaxed and reassured at the sight of me.

"Mum, are you okay? Do you have your tablets? What about the key to get into the flat?" She was allowed to give me her keys to the flat, so I could get in and see to the dogs and sort out how to fix this mess. I was worried about her medication and if she had enough tablets with her. A lady at the front desk tried to reassure me that everyone would receive a visit by a doctor, and if any medication was required, it would be administered. For some reason I wasn't convinced. I was in one of those situations where you really couldn't, or shouldn't, make too much of a fuss or demand too much; otherwise, you could be in trouble, or maybe make things more difficult for the person you are trying to help. I know that sounds like paranoia. I found out later it was nearly forty-eight hours before mum saw any medical staff, but luckily, she was okay.

I approached the lady at the front desk in the police station to find out what was going on, she told me mum would be taken to the women's prison in the morning. She suggested I talk to mum's solicitor as he would be able to tell me more. The lady had spoken, and that was it. There was nothing I could do for now; it was out of my control. Mum did seem fine all things considered; it was me who was the nervous wreck.

The solicitor would be my first port of call in the morning. I had already phoned him earlier that afternoon and told him what was going on. He was also very calm and collected but agreed to see me the following day to discuss the release of my mum. Mum had always spoken highly of him in the past, and she told me should she ever have any problems to go straight to him, Señor Garcia. He was expensive, but he always got the job done. I suppose everything has a price in this world.

Simon and I went back to the flat to get some much-needed rest and some food. I took the dogs for a walk and changed their newspapers. We called for a pizza to be delivered and we ate it half-heartedly. I was so shattered by this point, as soon as my head hit the pillow, I fell asleep.

My appointment with Señor Garcia was first thing in the morning around 9.30, I was there and waiting at nine on the dot.

I didn't want to waste any time and I had to make sure I was one step ahead of the game. I was working on speed, not the drug, but adrenalin. It was all moving at such a pace; I didn't want to miss a thing. I didn't want someone to turn around like they usually do and say, "You need to do this, but you should have done it an hour ago, now you have to wait till next week for the next chance." I couldn't afford to miss a trick. It was all down to me again.

"Señor Garcia, you have to help me. My mum's in prison and they say there were underage girls in the sauna, which isn't true. She only went down to help them with their enquiries, and they have put her in cells. You know she needs her tablets, and she always says how good you have always been to her in the past and how much she appreciates you. Please, you have to help her." Yes, I was desperate and pleading. If anyone was able to get her out of there, it would be him. I needed to see some action as there hadn't been any in the last two days.

He did seem flattered by all the compliments my mum had made about him, yet he still showed no sign of urgency. I suppose when someone does this sort of thing for a living, they may become immune to certain types of emotion. They may remain calm and collected, something I was far from. The lack of interest and urgency from those involved was starting to annoy me.

"I have made some calls and she will appear in court tomorrow morning at around 10.30, and then the judge will decide if she is to be released or not."

"What if he says no?"

"Then we can ask for her to be let out on bail." I couldn't take it all in.

"You can go and visit her later this afternoon if you want."

"I can? Where? When? How do I do that?" I was so out of my depth. This was a different world I had been fortunate enough never to have encountered.

"You need to be at the prison before three o'clock as you will have to queue to get a ticket, otherwise you won't get in. It is on a first-come, first-served basis, and only a certain number of people can visit in an afternoon."

"WHAT?" I exclaimed. I was going to be the first one in that queue, just watch me.

"I will go to the courts tomorrow and see what they say." And with that, it was clear the appointment was over.

I went to the sauna to see how everything was going, collect the takings and make sure all the girls were okay. I used the money to buy food and pay for the taxis back and forth. Everyone at work wanted to know what was happening and what the solicitor had said, so I gave them an update.

I gave Susi's husband a call and told him about my impending visit, and he insisted, quite rightly, he was going to come along as well. He would sort himself out and find his own way there. It was funny that I had never heard of these cousins before; now they had no money they appeared from nowhere asking for help and to borrow money. My mum was always willing to help others as she knew what it was like not to have any money, she was always prepared to give. After lunch, we went and stood outside the prison. It was the first time I had been this close to a prison, let alone going to visit someone inside who just so happened to be my mum. I had to wait for ages, not knowing if I was standing in the right place or what the protocol was. I was beyond nervous, and my eyes were swollen from so much crying, worrying about my poor mum.

Finally, we were called in through a door and into a narrow hallway with a receptionist at the end and a door to the left. I had no idea what to expect. I had taken my passport, and anything else I thought might be asked of me.

"What's your name? Who are you here to see?" Asked the lady

behind the glass window. I was so nervous I could hardly speak. I couldn't bear the thought of seeing my mum in a place like this. Perhaps if I closed my eyes, this would all go away. There's no place like home. There's no place like home.

"My mum." I gave her name and she looked down a list, then handed me a ticket with a number on it.

"When your number is called, you go through that door. You have fifteen minutes. Next!"

"Thank you, thank you."

Okay, she said when she calls this number I go through where? I have how long? I was trying hard to keep it together and remember everything. I couldn't believe this was happening.

I stood in line with the other people who were also visiting their family and loved ones and waited my turn.

Some numbers were called then mine. I followed those whose number had been called and we all went through a brown door into a small area with chairs placed in front of a booth. I had to sit in a booth which matched the number on my ticket. My mum wasn't there, where was she? The booth was enclosed so I couldn't even give her a hug or a kiss. I hadn't seen her for a couple of months, how was she going to cuddle me and tell me this was all one big mistake? Stop crying, I told myself, be strong, you silly cow, stop crying. The more I tried to stop, the more I cried. You only have fifteen minutes, make sure you say what you have to say. Do not waste it, I told myself.

Then a bell rang, she appeared and sat down in front of me, the other side of the reinforced window. The sight of her made me cry even more. She looked well and rested, the best she had looked in a long time.

"Mum, are you okay? Are they treating you well?"

"Oh, I'm being treated like a queen." I could not believe my ears. "Because I am the oldest of all the women in my cell, they are all looking after me as if I was their grandmother. One of the girls gave me her bottom bunk because she was worried about me climbing up on the top bunk. They are all young girls in here, you know. One of the girls is in because she stole a doughnut. I said she should have eaten the evidence. For a doughnut, can you believe it?" No, I couldn't believe it, my mum was treating this place as a holiday camp.

"The food is really good here, and everyone is so friendly." Here's me worried sick and she is living the life of Riley it seemed.

"Mum, I saw Señor Garcia, he is going to be at the hearing tomorrow." I started to cry again. I think it was mainly out of pure exhaustion.

"Evie, listen, in my bedroom there is my briefcase, and you need to open it. There is some money in there and some papers you need to take to the solicitor. There is a code for each side of the handle of the briefcase to open it." I knew what was coming next, I was going to have to remember these two codes. No pressure, like I don't have enough going on in my head at the minute. She gave me two lots of four different numbers, one code was for the right side and the other for the left. "Don't forget them, will you?" All I had to do was remember two sets of different code numbers like my life depended on it. Mum's life depended on it. I didn't have a pen and paper to write on as we weren't allowed to take anything in with us. "Right, do you remember the code?"

"I'll try." I kept repeating it and repeating it through my spurts of tears, but I wasn't sure I would remember it by the time I got back into the outside world.

"How is Susi doing?" I asked.

"Oh, she hasn't stopped crying since she came in here. She thinks if she keeps on crying, they will let her out. She is up in the infirmary, but she is alright. I tell you, if ever I become homeless, I would come in here. You get all your food and lodgings for free. We can watch television and play games." The bell went again to warn us we only had a few minutes left and to start saying our goodbyes. "Don't forget the codes."

"Okay, Mum, see you soon. Take care of yourself. I love you."

And that was it. Back outside, I felt so drained I needed a drink.

The next day I was waiting outside the courtroom for the judge's verdict. Was my mum going to come out today or in four months' time? Señor Garcia was nowhere to be seen. He said he would be here. If I could make it, why couldn't he? I kept pestering the courthouse receptionist who was taken aback with my forthrightness. I was demanding to be kept informed as if it were my right, and I believed it was. If you don't ask, you don't get.

"The trial hasn't finished yet, Señorita."

"Is my mum here within the court buildings? Will she be able to come home straight away?" I was in danger of being thumped by the lady or physically removed from the building by security if I didn't leave them to it. I made several calls to the solicitor in the meantime demanding to know where he was and why he wasn't here with me sorting this out. His secretary said he was busy and would be on his way over soon. Finally, after about half an hour, I went up to the lady again. This time she relented and told me mum was going to be allowed out on bail. What this meant precisely I wasn't quite sure.

Four million pesetas bail money and then she could be home in time for tea - the equivalent of £20,000!

I jumped into the first available taxi and was off. I had a mission to accomplish, and I knew exactly what to do. There was still no sign of the solicitor. Thankfully, it was only ten o'clock in the morning, and the banks wouldn't shut for another couple of hours. I had to race to the bank and pray the bank manager would let me take four million pesetas out of my mum's account without her authorisation and get it back to the judge before lunchtime. No problem then. The clock was ticking, and the solicitor was not answering my calls. I had accessed all this information on my own with no help from him whatsoever. What was he playing at? It was now Friday, and if I didn't get this sorted today, nothing would happen until Monday morning. Unbelievable! What was I going to say to the bank manager? He did know me, Mum had introduced us in the past. He had seen me many a time in the bank depositing money.

He had personally arranged money transfers over to my English account. No one would let me just stroll in and remove that amount of money, surely? I prayed to God for His help.

I rushed into the bank, the clock still ticking.

"Good morning, I need to see the bank manager please," I told the cashier, slightly out of breath. As I spoke, the bank manager came out of his office as if he had been expecting me. He walked towards me with an outstretched hand, ready to shake mine.

He then guided me into his office. On the table was the national newspaper, open at a page where the manager had just finished reading.

"Oh please, Señor, my mum is in jail for something she hasn't done, and I need four million pesetas to bail her out." How surreal and stupid did that sound.

"I know," he replied. He knew she was in jail, but he didn't know she needed bail money to get out. "I have just read it in the newspaper."

"You have?" I was astonished it was in the newspaper, albeit a small article, but it was there, nonetheless. "Please, can you help me? I need to get the money to the judge before one o'clock, otherwise she will be there all weekend!"

"Yes, no problem, just wait here and I will go and sort it out for you." As simple as that? I wondered how he was going to give me the money. Was he going to count that amount of money out in cash? Surely not. It had to be a special bank cheque or something. Fortunately for my mum, she had that amount of money sitting in her account, in one of her many accounts. He understood this was an emergency and knew I wasn't going to run off with it, and with a cheque payable to the courtrooms or judges or whoever, I wasn't going to get far. I couldn't believe how easy it had been. I guess my mum was his best client after all, and he knew she would be very thankful for his help in this matter. She would continue to bank there for a long time yet. The cheque was ready within ten minutes, and I was ready to jump into another taxi and continue racing against the clock. I thanked him so much and appreciated his concern and help. He had been the first one to show any sort of emotion since this whole thing started.

Once in the taxi, I told the driver to take the shortest route possible as this was an urgent matter. I encouraged him with the promise of a nice big tip if he could get me to my destination as fast as possible. We took the scenic route around the back of Montjuic and the Olympic stadium.

It was beautiful and calm up there, no traffic at all. I had a bizarre feeling of peace amidst all the rush and chaos around me. Down in the centre of the city all the cars were bumper to bumper so we would never have made it back to the courts in time before they closed had we not gone this way. As we were driving, I tried to get hold of the solicitor again.

"*Oh, hola*, Evie." What a surprise! I had finally managed to get hold of him.

"*Si, hola*, Señor Garcia." I was trying hard to keep my temper and not be rude to him as I knew I still needed him to sort out paperwork and the like. It was not over yet.

"Evie, I've just spoken to the judge" – as if he had been working hard on the case – "and your mum is being let out on bail."

"Yes, I know, for four million pesetas. I already know that, thank you. I have the money in my bag. I am five minutes away from the courthouse." I felt satisfied with myself. "And you are where exactly? Because if you are not there in five minutes when I arrive, I am not going to be happy." I was trying so hard to keep calm. If I said anything to upset him, it could all get a bit ugly.

"You already have the money?" This time it was he who couldn't believe what he was hearing. It seemed I wasn't supposed to know this information and maybe not be able to get hold of the money in time if at all.

"Yes, I have it all. The bank manager gave it to me. He knows me and the whole situation. I was at the courthouse first thing this morning, the lady told me what the verdict was." He was lost for words and defeated with no excuses but agreed to be at the courthouse in time to pay the money in before they closed for the weekend.

We met as agreed and walked to where the offices were. "I'm sorry but could you please walk a little bit faster, we don't have time to waste." Why was he lagging behind? Could he not walk faster?

We walked into the building which had marble floors and cool air-conditioning and I handed him the cheque. I hoped he wouldn't do a runner; I didn't trust him. I followed him wherever he went and listened in to what he said and to whom. He handed over the cheque and then handed me a receipt which I put safely into my purse. Was that it? Apparently so. Mum was now allowed out.

"When can I go and get her?"

"You'll have to go to the prison later on this afternoon after two o'clock."

"Is that it then? I don't have to do anything else? She will be released this afternoon?"

"Yes, that's it." He was keen to get out of there and on with the rest of his day and get some lunch no doubt.

Simon and I were there at two o'clock as instructed and waited by the doors together with a small group of other people who were also none the wiser of what was going to happen or when. There were two separate exits, and none of us were quite sure which exit they would come out of. I didn't want to miss her, I didn't want her to leave from one exit while I was standing like a lemon at the other, and she then jump into a taxi and go. We waited until six o'clock before anyone appeared. It all started to look a bit dubious. People were starting to mumble, "Look at the time, I can't see anyone being let out this late in the day. Nothing is going to happen now surely?"

It was starting to get dark, and I was so tired. Then, finally, there was some movement with doors opening, and people started to appear. Mum was amongst them. I ran to her relieved and gave her a big hug, but it wasn't the overwhelming reunion I had in my head. She was all jolly as if she had been on a little holiday having a good time, oblivious to the turmoil in which I had been living. We hailed a taxi and went home. I was stunned by the whole experience.

Chapter 11

Knights on Shiny Motorbikes

Pray continually.
- 1 Thessalonians 5:17 NIV

As I neared the age of sixteen, most of the girls in my English school, in my year all had boyfriends. Some of them even had one-night stands. I remember one of my friends boasted she was on boyfriend number fifteen! She was now pregnant. I didn't want to have a string of meaningless relationships, but I did want a boyfriend. So, at night before going to sleep I prayed for a boyfriend, not just any old boyfriend, someone who would be my best friend and lover, someone I would marry and live happily ever after with. I made sure the request was specific. I wanted a relationship that would last through thick and thin. Like the ones on the television where an old couple are being interviewed, and they tell you how they have been together for over fifty years. I prayed for someone I would adore and enjoy being with, and they would feel the same way about me. I truly believed Mr. Right was out there somewhere looking for me, Miss Right, we just had to find each other. I wanted a relationship full of affection, patience, understanding and sharing each other's dreams, wishes and values, a mutual love, physical and emotional. To my surprise, my prayers were eventually answered, I see it now. It did take many years for my knight in shining amour to appear, ten years to be exact, but as they say, all in God's timing.

Chapter 12

October 1996

For this reason a man will leave his father and mother and be united to his wife, and the two will become one flesh.
-Ephesians 5:31 NIV

Simon and I had recently split up. I had turned twenty-five and felt I was now standing at a crossroads. Was this what I wanted for the rest of my life? We had been together for nine years, no sign of an engagement ring or a wedding. He was such a nice guy and would do anything for me, he had a heart of gold, but unfortunately, I treated him like dirt. Deep down, I knew he wasn't the one for me. I wanted so much more out of life and a relationship. I wanted to go places and live life to the full. Life was for living and I intended to do just that. Don't get me wrong, I did love him very much, but as a friend, not as a lover, not with passion, I had so much passion to give but not to him. I was stuck in a relationship which had never been anywhere and was going nowhere. We were both stuck in a comfortable relationship like a pair of old comfy slippers. I knew I wasn't supposed to be where I was. Something kept telling me there was something better waiting for me around the corner. Something was about to happen in my life. A change was coming.

A few weeks later, in October, I was working for a promotional company marketing a rum-based drink through various pubs and nightclubs in London. It was a fantastic job. I visited all the best clubs and pubs, three venues a night, three nights a week, Thursday, Friday and Saturday. We had a great time meeting people and having a laugh, jumping in and out of taxis, being driven across the city of London, offering people free drinks, and to top it all you got paid for it. I was asked to be the team leader of a small team of four. Simon, with whom I had just broken up after a nine-year relationship, was the cameraman. James was a compere. Sue and I were the girls who went into the venue before the compere, to introduce ourselves and explain how the crew were going to come in, start filming and hand out free drinks for the best stories shared. James would come in and interview the people we'd selected and get them to say nice things about the product, which wasn't difficult as it was a popular product. People will tell you anything if it involves getting a free drink. James wore a brilliant sparkly spangled blue jacket with black velvet lapels. His appearance resembled something out of a 1970's TV talent show, complete with a giant microphone to interview people. Simon followed us everywhere with the camera recording the event, ready to convert it into a promotional video. We had such a laugh.

As the team leader, I was responsible for visiting the venues two weeks prior to the event and decorating the place with posters and bunting. There were over a hundred different venues. After each event, it was my job to return two weeks later, write a report on the success of the promotion and drop off a copy of the video we had made.

It was a Friday night in October, we went to Los Locos Tejas, a bar, restaurant, and nightclub, in Covent Garden. We had already been to two other venues, and we were now at our last one before heading home. The place was buzzing with people. It was a nice size venue with a capacity of about two hundred, and a fantastic atmosphere, very cosy with great music. Before 10.30 p.m., it was a restaurant serving great Tex-Mex food, and then the tables were all cleared away, and the lights changed, transforming it into a nightclub. You could see everyone was having a great time, drinking, singing, dancing, and when they saw us arrive the place became even livelier.

The job itself didn't take long, and we were only ever in a venue for no more than thirty minutes. It was run in, create a commotion, and run out again after having interviewed various people, handed out some free T-shirts and then leave. When the time was up, I went to look for the manager in charge for him to sign my paperwork and write down any comments. I went around to the back of the bar, but it was so busy, I struggled to get anybody's attention.

"Hello, is there a manager around? I need him to sign my paperwork," I shouted at the barmen, trying to be heard over the loud music and people ordering drinks, but they were too busy to notice me. I waited patiently while waiters and waitresses rushed in and out of the service area. A tall man walked past with dark wavy hair, very clean-shaven and looking very manager-like. "Excuse me, David, isn't it?" He walked right past me and looked back at me. "Can you sign my paperwork please?" I asked, holding it up.

"I'm busy, love, he'll sign it for you," pointing to another man standing right behind me. He also was tall and towered over me with distinguished greying hair and penetrating blue eyes. He was preoccupied with other things and was trying to avoid me. His assistant manager, David, had just dropped him into signing the promotional girl's paperwork. He was far too busy to be dealing with the likes of me. I stood in his way. "I'm really sorry. I know you're busy, but can you just quickly sign this for me? Then we'll be off." I shoved the paperwork under his nose before he had a chance to walk away from me. I didn't want to stand there all night.

"Yes, I suppose." Reluctantly, and with a sigh, he took my pen and paper without even looking at me apart from one quick glance. "So, how did the promotion go?" he asked, but wasn't really that interested, he was worried about the time and ensuring the tables were cleared off the dance floor ready for people to start dancing.

"Good, we had fun. It's a great place you have here. Let's hope you sell lots of bottles."

"Yeah, great." He started to move away.

"I'll be back in two weeks with the video. Thank you very much for having us." He was nice but obviously very busy dealing with customers. We gathered up all our things and went on our way.

The following night we continued our promotion. This time the venues were over in the Soho area. One of the venues was another bar, restaurant, and nightclub. I hadn't realised until we arrived that it was part of the same restaurant chain as the one we had visited the previous night. This one was much larger, called Los Locos Beach Club. I preferred it to Los Locos Tejas, they had the same menus, but the theme and decoration was different. This one had a Beach Club theme; the clue was in the name. The walls were covered with painted tropical beach scenes; palm trees, beach huts, a surfer's paradise. Again, the same as the previous venue, when 10.30 came around the lights switched from restaurant ambient to nightclub with painted walls coming to life with a fluorescent paradise island and palm tree landscape. This also was down in a basement, but one of the great features was the staircase. When you stood at the bottom of the stairs and looked up, there was an incredible 3D picture of a shark on the rise with its mouth wide open, giving the impression it was about to jump out and eat you. As the team and I waited at the bottom of the stairs, I looked up and saw a man right at the top. He was dressed in black motorbike leathers, and for some reason, I was transfixed.

I watched him as he walked down the stairs. He looked very tall and strong, he was gorgeous, and for some reason I couldn't take my eyes off him. I was captivated. I tried to stand in his way so he would notice me. It wasn't until he was halfway down the stairs, I realised it was the manager from the venue we were at the night before, with his greying hair and electrifying blue eyes. I couldn't and didn't want to take my eyes off him, which I thought was bizarre, but it was as if I was meant to just stand there.

"Hiya, how are you? It's us again. We were at Los Locos last night and we're here tonight." It felt weird, it felt like maybe he could be the one.

I was bound to meet someone at some point, how and when I didn't know, but it would have to happen eventually, but I was getting tired of waiting.

I had been single for about two months now, not my thing. He looked at me and removed two bottles of alcohol from inside his jacket and gave them to the manager. They had obviously just run out and this gorgeous guy was lending them some from his own stock. Wow! He was so tall and handsome, and he rode a motorbike, hence the leathers. Unfortunately, I hate motorbikes, they scared the heck out of me. Mum had done a good job at scaring the pants off me with tales of accidents and deaths she knew had happened to young people in Spain. I didn't dare go on one.

"Oh, hi there." He looked at me and then walked into the office. He must be a very shy person, I thought. Oh well, it wasn't meant to be. I then turned my attention to the job in hand, working and having fun.

I went back to the Los Locos Tejas venue two weeks later to see how the promotion had gone, hoping to catch a glimpse of the manager. Unfortunately, only David was working that night. "So, er, David? That other chap with the grey hair, he's not in today?" I enquired sheepishly.

"No, he's only gone and had a bad motorbike accident. He's in hospital at the moment." My heart skipped a beat.

"Oh, my gosh. How awful, that is terrible. Is he alright?" I was genuinely concerned.

"Yes, he'll be fine," relayed David confidently.

"Okay, well, tell him I said hello, and I hope he recovers soon."

I handed him the video and took notes on the amount of stock they had sold during and after the promotion and then I was ready to head to the next venue on my list.

"Right, that's me done. Thanks again for having us. Might see you again sometime." I said as I headed towards the door. And that was the end of that.

Chapter 13

April 1997

Listen to my words: "When there is a prophet among you,
I, the LORD, reveal myself to them in visions,
I speak to them in dreams."
-Numbers 12:6 NIV

One spring morning in early April, I awoke from a pleasant dream thinking to myself, wow, what was that all about? It was so weird, but good, at the same time. In the dream, I was having a drink with a man with grey hair. I couldn't see his face, but he was at a bar with me. His grey hair was so evident, I kept thinking to myself in the dream, I know I really like this man, but he has grey hair, he is far too old for me. I couldn't go out with someone that old. I'll just have this one drink with him now. He is really nice though and I do really like him, but I'm definitely not going to go out with him.

Later that day, while eating lunch in my part-furnished rented house, I received a phone call from one of the promotional and marketing companies I worked for. "Hi, Evie. How are you doing?"

"Very well, thank you. How are you? Do you have some more work for me?"

"Yes. We're running the same drinks promotion we did last year, and we wondered if you would be interested in being the team leader again with the same team."

"Would I? Yes, I'd love to, that would be great."

"Oh, thank you. I'll send all the relevant planning out to you today so you should have it by tomorrow along with the merchandise and point-of-sale products. It is the same brief as last time, so you won't have to attend any training sessions."

"Fantastic. When do we start?"

"In the next couple of weeks. So, if you can get the pre-merchandise up as soon as possible. You're not too busy at the moment, are you?"

"Nothing I can't work around. Don't worry, I will get it done."

"Cheers Evie. Speak to you soon."

This was exciting. I could work during the day on other jobs while merchandising in the same areas and do the drinks promotion at night after work. I could certainly do with the money. I contacted everyone from the team and checked if they were up for it and not busy on other jobs. They were all in and just as excited as I was. All the relevant paperwork arrived as promised the very next day. I was eager to see what venues we had and where they were. There were a few new ones in areas we hadn't covered before, and some we had. Obviously, since it was such a great event, they must have decided to repeat it. As I looked down the list, to my surprise, I saw Los Locos Tejas, the one we did last year. I had forgotten all about it, that was the one with the man with the grey hair. I couldn't remember a thing about him now, not even what he looked like, so much had happened since then.

I did my journey planning and filled the boot of my car with point-of-sale products and headed into London. I managed to park the car right outside Los Locos in Covent Garden, which was remarkable: to actually find a space! I headed downstairs carrying all the bits and bobs. "Hello, David, how are you?"

"You again? Are you doing that promotion again?" he said teasingly.

"Yes, that's why I'm here with all these goodies for you. Where do you want them?"

"Don't worry about it now, leave them here and I'll put them up later for you."

"Are you sure?"

"Yes, I've some other things up now which I need to take down anyway. I'll sort it out for you." Sounded like a plan, less work for me to do. I could finish sooner and beat the rush-hour traffic home. "When are you doing it?"

"Two weeks' time," I replied.

"Great, that James guy was so funny, he looked ridiculous in that jacket," laughed David.

"Yes, he did. Where is the other guy? The one with the grey hair. Has he left?" I assumed because I couldn't see him, he no longer worked there. It would be typical knowing my luck. I would have liked to say 'hi' and try to find out if he had a girlfriend - what his name was… Why was I even asking?

"Oh, Liam you mean. No, he's still in and out of hospital. He's had seven operations on his leg since his accident, he has had a few problems. He's in hospital now, but he should be out tomorrow."

Something stirred inside me, I couldn't believe what I was hearing. After all this time the poor guy was still in hospital. "He'll be okay. Why, do you fancy him or something?" David was now gently mocking me but meant no harm.

"No, I just wondered as he wasn't around, and it was he who signed my paperwork last time. Anyway, I'd better go. I really hope he feels better soon. Tell him Evie, the one with the brown hair, not the blonde one, says hello and I hope he gets well soon."

"Yeah, right. See you. I'll give him a ring now and tell him."

159

I wasn't sure if he was joking or not.

Two weeks later, I ran down the stairs into the same club to let them know we were getting ready. "David, we're just filming the introduction upstairs before we come down. Okay? We'll see you later and catch up with you when we're finished." I turned and ran back up the stairs to go outside when I heard footsteps running behind me.

"Evie! Evie!"

David was desperate to tell me something, but I couldn't hang around as the rest of the team were waiting for me. "Liam wants your telephone number!"

"What? I'm not giving him my telephone number. I don't give my telephone number out to anyone."

"Just so you know, I'm not allowed to let you leave without you giving me your number." He sounded adamant.

"I'm kind of busy right now. We'll talk about it after." I noticed Simon was hovering around me, eavesdropping on what David was saying.

"Don't give him your number. He probably only wants one thing."

"Don't be silly. What's it to you anyway? We're not together anymore, you know. I can do what I want." I was getting annoyed at having to justify my possible intentions to my former boyfriend.

"He's just going to use you." He was speaking more as a concerned friend, rather than a jealous ex. We were still friends, after all; nine years is a long time to be with someone.

"What do you know? He might just need someone to talk to. He's had a tough time." I honestly felt sorry for Liam, I wondered if he did have anyone he could talk to, after everything he was going through.

"I wouldn't if I were you."

"Well, you're not. Let's get on with some work, shall we?"

At the end of the evening, as I was about to leave, David came up behind me. "What's your number?"

"I can't give it to you." He was pestering me now. "Look, seriously, he told me not to let you leave unless I have a contact number." I couldn't believe this was happening. I thought about it for a short while. What if this poor guy just needed a shoulder to cry on after his ordeal? I'm twenty-five for goodness sake, and my life is just starting, how else am I going to meet new people and friends? And after all, it's only a number. I relented. "Okay, here you are."

"Great. You never know, you guys might be married this time next year or have babies." David was getting carried away now.

"No, I don't think so." I couldn't believe what I had just done, but I did feel very excited and adventurous. This was a guy I couldn't remember a thing about; all I knew was he had grey hair, and I liked what I saw when I last saw him. So that must be a good thing. Anyway, he probably would never call, though I hoped he would.

Sunday afternoon after returning home from walking the dog there was a message on my answering machine from a man whose voice I didn't recognise and whose name I couldn't make out either. It was him! I didn't think he would actually phone. I wasn't there to answer the call. What if he didn't call back? Why didn't he leave a number to call him back on? Oh well, tough, I suppose. I was so disappointed.

A couple of hours later the phone rang, and I jumped up to answer it. "Hello?"

"Hi, Evie? I'm Liam from Los Locos. David gave me your phone number." A shiver went down my spine, a good shiver.

"Oh, yes. Hi!" Play it cool. Play it cool, I told myself. "How are you? David told me you had a motorbike accident, and that was last year, and you're still in hospital."

"Well, yes, actually I have been in and out of hospital for the past six months. I've had to undergo seven operations."

"How awful! Why, what happened?" I was genuinely interested and concerned. Liam proceeded to tell me all about the accident, the how, where, when and everything since then and before. We talked non-stop for nearly two hours, at which point we were desperate to see each other. Neither of us remembered what the other one looked like, only that we liked what we saw at the time.

"So, how do you fancy going to The Beautiful South, next Sunday?" Liam asked. The Beautiful South sounded familiar, but I couldn't quite put my finger on what he meant. Must be a pub in London, I thought to myself. Try not to sound stupid as if you never go anywhere and you don't have a life; because you don't, but don't let him know that.

"Yeah, sounds great."

"Well, the concert starts at 7.30 so shall we meet for a drink first?" My head started to spin. Oh my gosh, he's inviting me to go to a concert with him. I didn't know if I had enough money. I was excited and worried at the same time.

"Oh. How much are the tickets?" I asked, playing it cool.

"I already have them, my treat. They'll only go to waste otherwise."

Oh, wow, he's paying for me to go to a concert. I wasn't used to this sort of extravagance. Sunday seemed such a long way away now for both of us. It was bizarre.

"Listen, I don't know if you're doing anything during the week, maybe we could meet up for a drink?" He's now proposing to meet up for a drink before Sunday. If he doesn't like me then at least he'll have time to take someone else.

"Well, I'm not busy Friday." I was just trying to go with the flow, which was turning more into a torrent than a flow now.

"Well, how about Wednesday?" He was keen as mustard. I was as nervous as anything without knowing why.

"Okay." We were both doing our best to act cool, but there was an underlying urgency in the air.

We arranged to meet in a pub in Watford, on Wednesday. I arrived on time, he was a few minutes late. It felt like I was on a blind date. I was a little worried wondering if he would even turn up. At least I knew he would be easy to recognise as he had grey hair and would be hobbling about on crutches. I dressed smart but casual and paid extra attention to my hair and make-up. I sat on my own for a while, then out of the window, I saw him being chauffeur driven by a friend. The friend rushed round to Liam's side of the car and promptly opened the passenger door for him and helped him with his crutches. Once he saw he was stable and hobbling confidently, he jumped back in the driver's seat and left him to it. I immediately rushed to the front door to hold it open for him, and there he stood, grey hair and blue eyes. He looked gorgeous. He looked at me and smiled. "Hi, I'm Liam."

"Hi, I'm Evie." We greeted each other with a kiss on each cheek and headed towards the bar. Liam ordered some drinks then we sat down. We talked and talked, Liam did most of the talking, which was fine by me. He must have been nervous because I didn't get to say much. At the end of the evening, I drove him back to his house, I left him to let himself in as I drove off down the road. We spoke every day on the phone for over an hour. A couple of days later we went for a meal to a French restaurant, followed by The Beautiful South concert. Six months later, we were married.

Chapter 14

Happy Birthday

Blessed are the meek, for they will inherit the earth.
-Matthew 5:5 NIV

In this afternoon's events, my life was catapulted into a completely different direction to which I thought it was happily heading. It was an event which had a significant effect on me then, and still does today: I wonder how different things could have been if I had only done one thing slightly differently. How different would my life have been? Life can change in an instant, sometimes for better and occasionally for worse. It's all a learning curve, a test at the end of the day. How we react to it is the question. Little did I realise just how much my life was about to change.

Mum was staying with us for a few days to celebrate Oscar's second birthday. I always looked forward to her coming to visit; but like any parent-child relationship, once the children have flown the nest, after a few days' things can start to feel uncomfortable, and arguments begin to take place. Things began to get a bit twitchy around the house.

It was Saturday afternoon, and the party was in full swing. James was now eight weeks old. Up until now, everything had been going as smooth as it could be – at least with a house full of mums and toddlers running around the place. James was still fast asleep, enjoying his afternoon nap in his room. My dad was sitting happily in the corner watching all the little ones trying to dance, bending their knees up and down having a little jig, but he was being careful they didn't get too close to him with their sticky hands. We finished playing 'Pass the Parcel' and all the other usual party games. The dining table was a mess, half-eaten food on 'Bob the Builder' party plates and bits of squished sandwiches and crumbs everywhere. Liam had just put the kettle on for another round of teas and coffees for the already exhausted mums. While waiting for it to boil, he placed the candles on the homemade chocolate cake which I had covered in Smarties. As if the children hadn't had enough sugar already!

Mum came downstairs from having a lie-down and walked past the kitchen door, heading for the living room. "Hi, Mum, would you like a cup of tea? Liam is just making some."

"Yes, that would be lovely. Thank you." She seemed a bit dazed by the number of people in the house. Some of them she had already met earlier and others I introduced to her there and then. "For those who haven't met my mum before, this is my mum." I announced. Everyone smiled and acknowledged her and said hello. "Mummy, remember Amanda, Joanne and Sue?" I quickly pointed out who everyone was and then left the room as I could hear James starting to wake up and making noises upstairs. As I went upstairs, I saw my cousin Cindy arrive and park her car on our drive. Something was wrong, it looked like she'd been crying. Mum and Cindy never really got on well with each other and I knew I had to forewarn Cindy that my Mum was here. I had to ask Cindy to be socially polite just for me; a tall order I know, but anything to try and keep the peace. I bumped into my mum as I was heading for the front door to see what was wrong with Cindy.

"Mum, James is crying. Could you please bring him down while I let Cindy in?" I went outside, and as I approached Cindy, she started to cry. "Whatever is the matter?" I asked.

"I've just come straight from a friend's funeral. It was awful, Evie, the whole family were in tears. I'm so upset."

"Well, go home. What are you doing here?"

"I wanted to see the birthday boy. I'll be alright."

"My mum's here."

"Oh, God! I'll be okay. I'll just say hello, politely. It's Oscar's birthday, and I don't want to spoil it for him."

"Come in and I'll get you a cup of tea." I led Cindy into the house and into the living room. Mum just handed James to me. Liam had finished making the drinks and was now ready with the candles lit on the birthday cake, about to walk in and sing "Happy Birthday". Mum was now in the living room with everyone else and Cindy. While I was in the kitchen checking we were all ready for the entrance of the cake, I heard the front door slam. "What was that? Who just left?" I asked, looking at Liam. I turned and looked out of the window to see Cindy walking down the drive in more tears than when she first arrived. I rushed out to her.

"What's happened? What's wrong?"

"I'm so sorry, Evie. I tried, honest I did. I just can't handle it today. She was so rude. There was no need for it. Normally I would have let it go over my head, but today I just couldn't take it. I'm so sorry." I was so confused, what was she going on about? She was really sobbing at this point. "Who said what?" As if I hadn't guessed already.

"Your Mum! I just walked in there and said hello to everyone, she turned around and said, 'This is Cindy. She has never liked me.' What a thing to say! I'm going now, I can't stay here."

"No, no, I understand. Please go home and get some rest. I am so sorry about this."

I was so angry with my mum at this point, but I couldn't say anything to her as always. I just walked in silently fuming at how she had upset Cindy so much; she pulls something like this every time just to get attention. Well, I had had enough of it. I wasn't going to pander to her antics anymore. I stormed into the house as lightly as I could, determined not to create a scene. Everyone was wondering what was happening. Mum came up to me. "What is the matter with her?"

"Oh, Mum, please leave it. She's really upset. She's in floods of tears. We'll talk about it later," I said as calmly as possible. "We're waiting to sing 'Happy Birthday'."

"Evie, are you ready?" shouted Liam from the kitchen, completely oblivious to what was unfolding.

"Yes, I'm coming." I wasn't going to let anything spoil my little boy's party.

And there it was, mum ranting "You always take her side. You always stick up for her, never me your poor old mum. Oh no, you prefer her to me. What about me? You don't care about me!" Then she stormed off upstairs.

"What was all that about?" Liam asked with his mouth open.

"Don't ask. I'll explain later. Right, have we got the candles lit? Are we ready?" Just as we were about to leave the kitchen, my mum came storming downstairs with her suitcase and handbag in her hand. "Mum, what are you doing?" She pushed past me and opened the front door. "Mum, where are you going? Don't be silly, stop it. Look, we're about to blow out the candles on Oscar's birthday cake."

"I'm going. How dare you treat me this way. It is always them over me. Well, I'm going back to my country and my people."

She started to walk down the road and I knew exactly what she was doing. I knew exactly what she wanted me to do and say, but I refused to do it this time. I was not going to play her game. Not today, not on my son's birthday. Not when I'm just about to sing "Happy Birthday" to him. I wasn't going to run down the road after her and say sorry for something I hadn't done, tell her how much I love her and beg her to come back into the house. Not in front of a house full of people. No, I wasn't having it. Not today. I was fed up with her mind games and her emotional blackmail.

So, I let her go. She was a grown woman, she had money and knew very well what she was doing. If she wanted to go back to Spain, then she was very capable of doing so on her own. I couldn't believe she had done this. How could she do such a thing? I was so upset, but I wasn't going to let it show. I was just so tired of it all, tired of having to put up with this for so many years.

I took James in my arms, and we went and sat down next to Oscar who was unaware of what had just gone on outside of the living room. "Right then! Are we ready, everyone?" I asked, trying to carry on as if nothing had happened. Liam opened the living room door and walked in singing, "Happy birthday to you, happy birthday to you…"

Mum didn't speak to me for ten months. She refused all my attempts to talk to her, shouting and swearing at me down the phone, as I tried to explain why Cindy had been so upset and that I hadn't been sticking up for anybody.

"You are dead to me now. Don't you ever call here again. I have changed my will. I am leaving you nothing, not a single penny. I never want to hear from you again. Do you hear me? Never!" And she hung up the phone.

Chapter 15

The Phone Call, Part 1

"Lord, how many times shall I forgive my brother or sister who sins against me? Up to seven times?"
Jesus answered, "I tell you, not seven times,
but seventy-seven times" -Matthew 18:21-23 NIV

"Yaya, it's me." Yaya is Spanish for nan; another term for calling someone grandmother. My grandmother answered the phone. At first, she strained to recognise who the caller was. As she got older and slightly hard of hearing, I wondered if she could hear me or if she even remembered who I was. I hadn't seen her in nearly two years, the last time being when I was thirteen weeks pregnant with James. Because flying when pregnant isn't recommended, depending what stage you're in, my visits were few and far between; especially because of my fear of flying. As my heart would beat faster than usual, I worried how that might affect my baby's little heart.

My poor old yaya who lived in Spain, still hadn't met her second great-grandson, so I made sure I called her every other week to give her updates on how he and his older brother were getting on. She never went anywhere or did anything different from one day to the next, so our conversations always followed the same pattern, covering the same ground every time.

"*Hola?* Hold on a minute. I can't hear you very well. Let me go into the other room and pick up the phone there." Before I could reply she was already halfway to the other phone.

"Are you there? *Hola?*" I could imagine her pressing the buttons on the phone to see if it was connected properly. "*Sí, sí*, I'm here, Yaya."

"Good. Good. Anyway, how are you, Evie?"

"I'm fine. I've just come back from collecting Oscar from playschool, and we were just about to have some lunch. How are you doing?" I knew exactly what the answer was going to be. It was the same every time.

"Not too bad. I'm here watching television. I feel much better, a little tired, but I'm alright. It's just old age." She would say she was feeling better, not knowing I was unaware of her not feeling well in the first place.

If things weren't going well for her, she wouldn't tell anybody so not to worry them. Consequently, it would come as a shock and concern when you did find out. "How is everyone?" I was wondering how my aunt and uncle were. They lived two floors above my nan, which was a good thing for her, as my uncle came down every morning and evening to sit with her for twenty minutes and watch some television. He would have a moan about one issue or another and then go back upstairs. His wife, my aunt Pilar was a sweet, gentle little lady who was probably no taller than five foot two. She always greeted you with a smile and had a very laid-back attitude to everything, a very traditional Spanish woman who dedicated her life to looking after her husband, children, and her home. She was always happy to offer unsolicited advice and tell you things as they were. I remember her saying to me when I was little, "You're my only niece, that is why your aunty loves you, and when you get married, your aunt is going to buy your wedding dress." I was touched by the show of affection, but as it turned out when I did get married, she wasn't even at the wedding. My dad paid for my wedding dress, which I chose 'off the peg' as they say, from a sale in Debenhams. It wasn't the most expensive in the showroom or the cheapest. It was just what I was looking for. Not too plain or simple, not too much of a meringue. What made it special for me were the twirly bits at the bottom of the dress, like those on a Spanish flamenco dress. I chose it as a tribute to the Spanish side of my family. Mum didn't talk to her brother or his family anymore - hadn't done for about ten years, which meant I wasn't supposed to be seen to be talking to them either or asking how they were. However, whenever I went to visit my nan, I would sometimes sneak upstairs and say hello to them all. Yaya would encourage it, so there were no bad feelings after I'd left, and she wouldn't have any awkward conversations. Last year my aunt found a lump on her breast and had a mastectomy two weeks later. Yaya kept me up to date with her health checks and thank God she was doing okay.

"Yes, everyone's fine."

"That's good." I knew we were coming to the end of our conversation. We had covered all the usual formalities, and I was wondering whether there was anything else I could add before saying goodbye. Then Yaya continued. "But I will tell you who hasn't been very well lately, your mum." Suddenly, I felt cold. I tried not to talk about mum too much as I would normally end up getting upset. Yaya had given up ages ago trying to make my mum see sense and get her to talk to me again, trying to convince her to take my calls. I usually asked how she was doing, but I hadn't done in the last couple of calls.

Every time Yaya tried to talk to her about me, my mum would erupt like a volcano. This in turn upset my yaya. My mum didn't want to have anything to do with me ever again, I was used to it. I didn't care, at least I was stress-free and relaxed, not having to wonder whether I was going to say or do the wrong thing and afterwards wonder whether I had done it on purpose or to spite my mum. No more guilty conscience. No more emotional blackmail. I no longer carried the weighty sensation around with me. I was getting on with my life, and she with hers.

Yaya told me of a conversation she'd had a few weeks ago with my mum. She had had a coughing fit and started to cough up blood, quite a bit seemingly, so she went to the Emergency Department worried, and was told she had burst a small blood vessel, but everything was okay. She had soon stopped coughing and the blood disappeared. I checked the story over again with my nan to make sure I had understood everything correctly and that my mum since then hadn't had any repeat episodes and was fine. Although I was worried for mum and her state of health, nan assured me it was just a cough and a little cold, and she was now back to normal and feeling well, so I didn't pursue it any further. There was no need for a phone call to my mum to see if she was alright. I couldn't bear having the phone put down on me again and to be reminded how much she hated me and how she didn't want me to call.

"She still has trouble with her bronchioles. It's because she won't give up smoking and she never will. You can't tell her anything. She won't listen." The words were coming out of my nan's mouth like a steam train with no brakes. She just kept going on and on; why couldn't she just stop talking so I could get on with my day? "They found a shadow on her lung, and the doctor told her, if she doesn't give up smoking, she only has six months to live, but she won't listen. She says she's given up, but I don't believe her. You can hear it in her voice, all that whistling noise." At this point, I was sitting on the floor in the middle of my living room, my whole world spinning around

173

me. I was unable to move. I wondered whether this was another of yaya's, "Well, with you and your children being so far away I didn't want to worry you" scenarios, or maybe my mum had told her not to say anything to me. I thought the best thing to do was not to sound as if I were about to panic, just in case my yaya slowed down and stopped giving out more information. So many thoughts were racing through my head, but Yaya just kept going.

"She has to go for a biopsy or something, to see what it is all about." My nan finally said all she had to say, and we said our goodbyes. As usual, I promised to call again soon, and that was that. I sat dazed on the living room floor like a rabbit caught in the headlights, when I had a beaker thrust into my face.

"Mummy, Mummy, I want some juice." Oscar was demanding some attention along with his baby brother, not far behind, in desperate need of a tissue.

"Okay, okay. I'm coming, darling."

I couldn't believe what was happening. I knew perfectly well what a shadow on the lung meant. My English nan had had one when I was sixteen. I knew what it was. I had already lived through the same experience fourteen years ago. What was happening? I felt as if my world was caving in on me. This did merit a phone call, an urgent one. If I was told to get lost, then at least I can say my conscience was clear and I had tried. When I had a quiet moment, I phoned Liam at work to tell him what had been said. He was just as shocked as I was. He did his best to console me over the phone but had to go as he had deliveries turning up at the front door which needed to be checked and signed for. I could hear the phones ringing in the background. If there was anything to be said it would have to wait until he got home. The rest of the afternoon and evening went by in a blur. I felt as if I had been thrown down a precipice and was on a rollercoaster of emotions, just like when my English nan was dying of cancer.

My heart was racing as I dialled the numbers. I misdialled at first as I hadn't called for ages. I called dad quickly to check I had the right number. I hoped he wouldn't ask why I needed it, which he was bound to, I could never ask him for anything without him enquiring what it was for.

Thankfully, he didn't ask. How could I forget my own mother's phone number? I used to dial it nearly every day. As the phone was ringing, I was aware of the stillness in my bedroom. My breathing was loud, and my heart was pounding. I wondered what sort of reception I would get. Would it be "Get lost, don't call here again." Or maybe, "how could you do this to me? You are a wicked daughter. God will punish you." These were all the usual torrents of accusations my mum would sometimes shout at me throughout my life, I was used to it. I was ready for whatever abuse she decided to throw at me. I just wanted to talk to her to make sure she was alright.

Was there anything I could do? Several months had passed since Oscar's birthday party when she ran out of the house. I hadn't spoken to her properly since. I rehearsed what I was going to say and how I was going to say it. Part of me was hoping there would be no answer, then at least I could say I called, but this was a serious matter for which I had to get the facts.

The ringing tone stopped, and I heard my mum's voice for the first time in a year. Stay calm, I told myself. I missed the sound of her voice; I missed my mum.

"*Mama*, it's me." There I had done it, that wasn't too bad. Maybe I sounded a bit too serious, but I had managed to make the first move. I could breathe now.

"*Oh, hola.*" A cold, slow, 'not very bothered to hear from you, but was expecting you to call sooner or later' tone of voice replied. At least she hadn't put the phone down on me yet.

"Yaya tells me you haven't been well lately. She mentioned something about you going into hospital for a check-up on your lungs?" I tried not to let on exactly how much information I was aware of. I wanted my mum to tell me in her own words.

"Yes, I was in the Emergency Department a few weeks ago because I had a coughing fit and was coughing up a lot of blood. The doctors told me I had burst a small blood vessel. They took some X-rays and they found something on my lung, and I need to go for a biopsy next Tuesday."

"Aha, right. How do you feel?" I enquired.

"Oh, I feel fine. I feel as fit as a fiddle. The only thing is I have trouble breathing, and I cough a lot sometimes, but I feel fine." As she breathed, I could hear she sounded wheezy and rattling, which took me back to my dying nan's bedside. This didn't sound good, it didn't feel right.

"Listen, Evie…" Her tone changed to a more challenging voice as if she were about to enter into a verbal war. Okay, this is it, I'm ready for it but I just wanted to be there for her. I held my breath, I could take it. All I had to do was hang up the phone at the end and forget about it. Not a problem. I've been through this so many times in the past. It starts off with her talking to me all nice and sweet, lulling me into a false sense of security, and just when I think everything's okay… bang! But they are just words, words don't hurt too much.

"I just wanted to say I'm really sorry for how I've treated you while you were living here in Spain. I did some nasty things which I shouldn't have done, but I'm sorry."

Sorry!? My mouth dropped open and I was speechless.

"I know there are things I have done which you haven't agreed with, things you didn't like. I did them not because I am a bad person, because I'm not, it is because of how I was brought up with the nuns, and that is the way I am. You never told me how you felt at the time. Why did you never tell me 'Mum, you're embarrassing me,' or 'Mum, you shouldn't do things like that."

I was desperately trying to understand this confusion and the amazement of my mother saying sorry to me for the first time ever.

"Well, I never said anything because you never listen to a word I say, so I reached a point where I knew it was better to say nothing." I kept asking myself, was this a wind-up? Was my mum about to turn round any minute, and say "you must be joking, me apologise to you? For what?" Was she trying to call my bluff in some way? I couldn't see how that would be possible since I didn't have any bluff to call.

"I have done a lot of thinking over the last few weeks and, I know I have cancer, so if I'm going to die, I just wanted to say sorry."

I was even more shocked she had been thinking about all of this over the last few weeks. She must have been feeling guilty. It wasn't me after all these years. I thought I had been the cause of all her suffering. I was the evil, mentally disturbed child, the one God was going to punish for so many things I had done in my life. I had been given a pardon, - 'not guilty, your Honour.' A huge rush of emotion came over me. My mum had said something I had waited thirty years to hear. Part of me wanted to be her little girl again and run into her arms like I used to and give her a big cuddle and kisses, but the other part of me was still weighed down with the bitterness and resentment which had slowly built up over the years and now seemed to be stuck fast. I wondered if I would ever be able to open my heart again the way she so desperately needed me to. If I did, would it get damaged again?

"Mum, you don't need to say sorry." Was that what she was expecting me to say? How do I follow that?

"You know I love you, Evie."

"Yes, I love you too, Mum, but you're not going to die. Everything will be alright." I was trying to say what I thought was the right thing, and not what I really felt.

"Do you think so?"

"Of course I do."

"Anyway, how are the boys?" asked Mum.

"They are well, they're fast asleep. You should see James. He looks just like me. Brown eyes and brown hair, very Spanish-looking. Oscar still has his beautiful blonde hair and gorgeous blue eyes. They're so beautiful, Mum."

It seemed weird describing my sons' appearance to their own grandmother. Usually, grandparents know what their grandchildren look like, how they act and what they get up to. She hadn't seen them since Oscar's second birthday when James was only eight weeks old. There had been a few changes since then.

"Well, give them a kiss from me. Anyway, there's a good film about to start on the television I want to watch."

"Yes, okay. I must go now anyway. I'll give you a ring next week, if that's alright with you, to see how you get on with the biopsy."

"Okay, Evie. I'll speak to you soon."

"Speak to you soon, Mum, look after yourself." I cried in disbelief and total confusion.

Chapter 16

The Phone Call, Part 2

They will have no fear of bad news; their hearts are steadfast, trusting in the LORD. -Psalm 112:7 NIV

A few days later, I phoned mum, just like I said I would, to see if she had received the results from her biopsy. It was confirmed – bronchial cancer. She was due to start having treatment within the next couple of weeks, a mixture of chemotherapy and radiotherapy. I worried about how she would cope on her own. Who was going to look after her while she was recovering from her various treatments? I had heard so many different stories about side effects from the medication, sometimes making the patient feel worse than the illness itself. I would have to go over there and live with her full-time. How was I going to manage with two small boys? I had so many different scenarios running through my head, but which one would be the best for us as a family? Not forgetting my husband still had a business to run. How advanced was this thing? Would she make a recovery? What would happen if she didn't recover? How could I be with her? She mustn't be on her own, she shouldn't die alone. Her main fear had always been dying alone while I was in England and no one finding her until it was too late. I wasn't going to let that happen. I wanted to be with her, support her while she was having her treatments. How was I going to manage that?

"Mum, how are you feeling?"

"Okay. It's okay. I know I have cancer but it's okay. I have done what I have done in my life, and I don't regret it. The Doctor has given me a lot of tablets to take, and I have an appointment for my chemotherapy session in a couple of weeks." She was pragmatic. "It is what it is." She said in an accepting tone.

"Mum, do you want me to come over and be with you? I can fly over and stay with you for a few days."

"No, it's okay, I have spoken to Nuria, and she said she would come with me."

"If you're sure?" Mum still seemed a bit reluctant, a bit hesitant with me, and still not wholly relaxed with talking to me, as if nothing had gone on in the past ten months. "Mum, listen. Liam and I are going to spend New Year's Eve at a theme park in France with the boys, we're driving down. If you wouldn't mind, we'd love to come and see you. The boys would love to see you and then I can come with you to a couple of your appointments."

"What? You would drive down to Spain?" She sounded surprised.

"Yes, we'd really like that."

"Are you sure Liam wouldn't mind, it's a long way? What about his work?"

"It's Christmas, he's on holiday. He can take as much time off he wants as long as he gives enough notice."

"Yes, that would be nice." My mum's voice began to show signs of excitement, but she was trying hard to restrain it. She didn't want to seem too keen.

"Right then, that's settled. We will be with you on New Year's Day." I was excited now, and I couldn't wait for my mum to see the boys. I knew she had missed them, what a time to reconcile.

New Year's Eve was a mixture of new beginnings and endings of chapters. We had a fantastic time at the Park. Oscar was running around with the biggest smile on his face at the sight of all the magical lights, sounds and smells of the Park. With the magic of the parades and the sight of the largest, most beautiful, Christmas tree I had ever seen, standing proud in the main square, I found myself crying, overwhelmed with emotion as I admired its beauty. This would always be a special place for me. I had worked there for a summer season eight years before and had made so many great friends and had so much fun. It was so special to be able to bring my own children and share this extraordinary place with them.

James had just learnt to walk but hadn't yet learnt direction, walking in a straight line was challenging. Not wanting to restrict him, we spent most of the time following him from behind, zig-zagging left to right and then going back on himself. He was so cute. The only thing to slightly dampen our spirits was the weather. It was freezing cold, and fog covered us like a protective blanket. Snow had fallen enhancing the whole atmosphere, turning the Park into a winter wonderland. Both boys looked like two walking marshmallow men, wearing thick snowsuits along with hat, gloves, scarves and complete with snow boots. Some may call me an over-protective mother, but at least my children were not cold, maybe a little on the warm side but not cold. Unfortunately, when night-time came, the long-awaited New Year's Eve fireworks display was called off due to the fog. We didn't mind, the boys were exhausted from the amount of fun they'd had throughout the day. They had fallen asleep in their beds while waiting to return out into the cold. Oscar was tired from trying to stay on his feet whilst learning to ice skate on the makeshift ice rink which had been especially created for the winter season. He was so funny, bless him. He enjoyed every minute of it, I just wanted to head back to the hotel where we were staying, out of the cold. Liam and I snuggled up in our large comfy bed and saw in the New Year watching television instead, enjoying treats from the minibar. Despite the lack of fireworks, we still had a fantastic time.

The next day we packed up the car and began our slow and steady drive down to Spain. At that time of year driving through central France and over the Midi-Pyrénées can be hazardous. There tends to be lots of snow, with poor visibility due to continuous fog. We took it nice and easy listening to 'Bob the Builder' and other popular children's songs at that time, over and over and over again.

On arrival at mum's flat, it was as if nothing had happened between us, and there was a massive welcome for her two grandsons. "Oh, come in, come in. Hold on, let me just switch off the television."

In the phone calls running up to our visit, mum was clearly mellowing out and was really looking forward to seeing us and the boys. I did wonder whether things would flare up again, remembering her last walk out. If necessary, I knew to just keep my mouth shut and agree with everything. Things were slightly different now, I was visiting my mum, and she had cancer. God was going to have to do a lot of work.

"Look at you, Oscar! Aren't you a big boy now? Look at your gorgeous blue eyes and your blond hair." Her heart melted when she saw him. She was so proud of him. I let her finish fussing over Oscar and then reintroduced James to her. "And this is James." James was now thirteen months old and walking since the last time she saw him. "Hello, James." She started to cry tears of joy and gave them both big hugs and kisses.

"I have bought them some toy cars. I hope that is alright? and some colouring pens for them to do colouring."

"Of course it is Mum." She went and sat down on the sofa and watched Oscar and James while they explored their new surroundings.

"I thought tomorrow we could go shopping and buy them some belated Christmas presents because I haven't bought them anything yet. I didn't know what to get them."

"Yes, they will love that."

"Would you like a cup of tea, and you Liam, you must be exhausted after all that driving?"

The children were the focal point for the rest of the evening. "What would the boys like to drink? Do they want some dinner? I bought them some of those nice children's yoghurts. You know the small ones, they're very nice you know. I had one myself, they're full of calcium."

"Thank you, Mum. I'll sort something out shortly." Mum sat and admired the boys.

The boys approached mum's wall cabinet where all her precious ornaments were displayed, her framed photos, crystal glassware, along with her collection of porcelain and china objects. "Oh, darling, no, you mustn't touch those. Those are Yaya's things, and they are very fragile. You play with your toys. Look at this car."

"Yes, Oscar. Don't touch those. You can look at them, but you mustn't touch them, they might break. Good boy." Oscar walked away from the unit and decided to see what James was up to instead.

A couple of days later, mum had an appointment with her oncologist, and she wanted me to go with her, which I was happy to do. The oncologist was very upbeat towards mum and told her how she was going to send her for a few more sessions of chemo and then radiotherapy. She sent mum to get undressed ready for the check-up, and while she was behind the screen, the oncologist and I were trying to whisper to each other.

"Is she going to be alright?" I whispered, trying to be discreet and to establish how poorly mum actually was and what was the prognosis. I had been trying to make an appointment with the doctor for a few days previously - but to no avail. I needed to know, living in another country; I had to make plans. Was I going to have to move in with my mum so I could take care of her? Was she going to be okay? I didn't want to worry about the unknown. The oncologist kept talking to mum as my mum wouldn't stop asking questions which weren't really relevant to the appointment, so I wasn't able to have a proper conversation with the doctor who just looked at me and shook her head. What did that mean? I wasn't sure.

"Right, these results seem fine. Come back after you've completed the next sessions and we'll take another look then."

"You know, Evie, this doctor is the best. Pedro gave me her details. He told her to look after me." She was making the doctor blush a little.

"Yes, your nephew has phoned for an update on your progress." Nephew? What nephew? Mum didn't have a nephew!

Back at home, mum explained, "Oh, Pedro had to say he was my nephew; otherwise, she wasn't allowed to give him any information about me. It is thanks to him she is dealing with me. How nice of him."

"Mum, I was thinking, why don't I come and move over here for a while and look after you? You need looking after while you have your treatments, someone to cook your meals and keep the house tidy. I could come over with the boys and stay in one of the other flats, that way you won't be tired all the time and you'll be able to get some rest."

"Both flats are rented out."

"Well, tell one of the renters they need to leave because your daughter needs to come and look after you." She thought about it for a bit. I could see she wasn't averse to the idea.

"I can't. Pedro has some friends living in them, and I can't tell them to leave."

"Of course you can, he'll understand." I couldn't see it being a problem. She thought some more.

"No, it's okay. I'll be alright. Nuria said she will come when I have appointments, and I am fine for the moment anyway. You have the boys and Liam to look after. You have to take care of your family."

"Mum, I can send the boys to the local nursery during the day and then they will be learning Spanish, which will be brilliant for them. Then at night, I'll be in the flat just across the road, so if you need anything, all you have to do is just pick up the phone."

"I can't just tell them to leave."

"Okay, fine, but if you start feeling poorly, I'll have to come over and then you'll have to arrange something." I was feeling frustrated: for some reason, she was reluctant to vacate one of the two flats, which, (news to me) were currently being rented out to Pedro's friends.

"Yes, alright." I knew she wanted me there, she didn't want me to go back to England. But my life had to carry on. I was at college studying complementary therapies, which I enjoyed very much, but I was happy to put everything on hold to look after her.

I returned a couple of times over the following months, and mum loved my visits. I went with her to as many appointments as possible.

185

I was desperate to know what progress mum was making, if any. One afternoon we hailed a taxi and went to visit the radiotherapist. The boys came with us, and we would all wait in the waiting room. The session only took a couple of minutes, with minimal after-effects just a little bit of tiredness. I was hoping to speak to her radiotherapist as mum had told me how nice and funny he was. I tried again to meet the oncologist privately but still with no success due to her busy schedule. Mum wanted me to go and find out exactly what the prognosis was and was happy for me, as a concerned daughter to ask questions. I sat nervously with the boys in the waiting room watching all that was going on around me; people with deadly diseases hoping and praying to be cured. I was hoping to catch the attention of the radiotherapist.

I was praying for some help. I needed to talk to someone, yet there were no doctors around, only nurses coming and going. Then a man with dark wavy hair, wearing a white coat and carrying a file came towards me.

"Are you the daughter of Señora Santiago?" Mum was right, he was nice and spoke softly and calmly, whereas I, on the other hand, started to get even more nervous.

"Yes."

"Come with me," he said softly, looking around, checking no one was listening. I was surprised, instead of me going looking for him, he came looking for me.

"Listen, Oscar, James, we're going in to talk to the doctor, and we need to be very good and try to be as quiet as we can, okay? You be good boys for Mummy."

The doctor was waiting for us to enter his office. He was happy for the boys to be there and judging by the photographs on his desk and wall he was a family man himself. His office was relatively small with a highly polished wooden desk along with a big leather chair in which he was now sitting. Next to him on the wall was a screen for examining X-rays.

I was wondering if my mum was out yet, and if so, was she looking for me, wondering where I was.

"Are you aware of your mother's condition?"

"Well, yes, but not entirely. I have been trying to speak to her doctor, but I can't get an appointment."

"She isn't very well," he said. Okay, I can cope with this I thought.

"Her cancer has advanced. It is well into her lungs now."

"Right, and what does that mean?"

"It doesn't look good. If you look at this last X-ray, you can see these patches here and here."

Was he saying what I thought he was saying? What was he saying? Tell me exactly what you're trying to say to me, I was screaming in my head at him.

"It's not good news." He said finally.

"Is she going to…?" I couldn't bring myself to complete the question.

"I can't give you a time." Oh my gosh, he is serious! I thought to myself.

"Well? What do you mean? What are we talking about, a year? Eight months?"

"I'm not God. I can't give you a time, but the way things look at the moment, Christmas if she's lucky."

"Christmas? What, this Christmas?" He nodded. Oh my gosh! I thought. I felt dizzy, I felt sick. I looked at my boys playing quietly on the floor and behaving so well. They were such good boys. But Christmas was only a few months away. He must be mistaken. She's been doing so well. Yes, a large lump had appeared on the side of her forehead, and they had given her some radiotherapy to stop it growing but not this, he must be wrong.

"Do you have any other family?" He asked.

"No, I'm an only child and my parents are divorced. It's good that you have told me because I need to make plans, like moving my family here so I can be with her."

"I think that's a good idea. Just make the most of it. She's a strong lady and has a lot of character."

"Yes. Thank you so much. I had better head back before my mum starts looking for me."

"Yes. I will call her in to have a chat when she comes out."

"Thank you so much for talking to me Doctor." I was so grateful for his time and the concern he showed me, and just as we reached the waiting room, mum came out looking a little confused. "Mum, are you alright?"

"Yes, that was weird. Do you know what the nurse asked me?"

"No?" I was still trying to grasp what I'd just been told by the doctor.

"She said, 'Oh, Señora Santiago, when did you have your lung removed?' I said I haven't had my lung removed. She was shocked then she told me that one of my lungs had collapsed. That explains why I have been a bit more out of breath."

I tried to keep calm for mum's sake. How dare the nurse just blurt something out like that without any diplomacy. We went and sat down, waiting for the doctor to call her in for a quick consultation. Within minutes we were called. Mum put on her shy, flirtatious face in order to impress the doctor.

"Hello, Doctor. Isn't he a nice, good-looking doctor, Evie?" He just laughed and asked us to take a seat. Before he had a chance to say anything, mum started, "Well Doctor? How am I doing? Am I getting better? Tell me I'm getting better, Doctor, because you can see what beautiful grandsons I have. I want to go to their weddings." Talk about how to make things awkward for someone.

Mum didn't waste any time. She knew what she wanted to hear and what she didn't, and even if you told her the truth, she would pretend she hadn't heard it.

"Señora Santiago, you have a beautiful daughter and two fantastic grandsons. The best thing you can do is to relax and enjoy them as much as you can, make the most of your family." What a nice way to say you're dying, figure it out yourself. Listen to the cryptic answer no one really wants to hear or believe.

Mum just smiled at him and repeated, "I want to go to my grandsons' weddings. They have come to visit me. I love them so much. They are so good, you know."

"You need to enjoy your beautiful family." It seemed as if she wasn't really listening to him. He didn't even talk about the latest X-rays. Everything was said that needed to be said. I had so much to do, but how was I going to do it all? Mum seemed oblivious to her condition, but she would want to know. She had her business to sort out, windup or at least close down. There were places she would like to visit now we had the prognosis. She wouldn't take it lying down, and she wouldn't want to be on her own. How was I supposed to deal with all this? What was I supposed to say? I needed to talk to Liam as soon as we arrived back at the apartment.

Back at the apartment I made us both a cup of tea and left mum to relax on the sofa while I went and gave the boys a bath and prepared them for bed, then I started to make dinner for us. I thought now was a good time to bring up the suggestion of me moving back to Spain.

"No, I don't think Pedro would agree to it because he has the flats occupied."

"Mum," I was getting very frustrated now, "I don't care. What are you so worried about? They are your apartments, they belong to you and I'm your daughter. Where is he now? You called me when you weren't well, and I came all the way from England to be with you."

"He's a very busy man." I could feel myself starting to get annoyed. Something wasn't right.

"What about his wife?" I was starting to really get upset. I knew I had been disinherited, and as I said, I didn't care. My conscience was clear. She had left it all to Pedro because he had helped her so much, but where was he now when she needed him most?

"Well, you know, she has to work and is also busy." I lost it there and then. Something really was wrong here.

"Mum, I'm sorry, but I have two small children, I'm doing a college course studying five different subjects and live abroad. They live just across the road and have grown-up children, and they never come to see you. There is something not quite right here. I'm here, Mum! Where are they?"

I had struck a chord, and she went quiet. She knew I was right, but she wouldn't admit it.

"I'm going to talk to Pedro, you need someone to be with you to look after you. If it isn't me, then I'm going to get someone to come and live in so they can take care of you, okay?"

"Okay."

"We'll sort something out before I go back to England in the next few days. I will get something organised. Otherwise, I'm not leaving you on your own." Shortly after, the phone rang. It was Pedro.

"Let me talk to him," I mouthed to mum. By now she was too tired to argue.

"Pedro, Evie would like to say hello to you." She passed the phone to me and went into the kitchen to make herself a cup of tea. Now was my chance and I had to make the most of it. I was so concerned. I knew he would be too.

"Hi, Pedro. How are you?"

"Yes, very busy, very busy." That was his default response.

"Listen, I need to talk to you. Are you able to ask your friends to vacate one of the flats across the road? I need to come over and look after Mum."

"Why?"

I needed to tell him, he needed to know the situation. I made sure mum was out of earshot.

"I went to the doctors with mum today, and the radiotherapist had a quick word with me. Look, he told me mum is really poorly and only has until Christmas if she's lucky."

"What! What are you saying? Who told you that?" His attitude shocked me completely. Why was he shouting at me down the phone? Why was he having a go at me?

"What did he tell you?" I felt like I was being interrogated.

"I just told you, she's not well, and she only has until Christmas, I need to be here with her to look after her." I was starting to get angry with his extraordinary reaction towards me.

"How dare he tell you that! It has nothing to do with you!" For some reason, he was angry. Was I hearing this man correctly?

"I beg your pardon. What do you mean? Of course it has everything to do with me. I'm her daughter!"

"It's a professional secret. No one is supposed to know about that sort of stuff." He was so angry and now shouting at me. I wasn't quite sure, but maybe this was the Spanish way of doing things.

"What are you saying? In England, you have to know these things so people can prepare themselves."

"What do you mean 'prepare themselves'?" What was this guy on? I didn't understand anything, any of it. "Mum has a lot of things she needs to sort out; she has a business that she needs to get in order, she has paperwork to sort. She needs to know."

"Don't you dare tell her. They shouldn't have told you anything, it's a professional secret. Don't you tell her anything!" Maybe he was right. Perhaps this was how they did it in Spain, maybe he knows of a different way of doing things.

"Anyway, I need access to one of the flats so I can come over with the kids to look after her."

"No, you don't need to. She's fine. The children would just tire her out. She wouldn't want you around. You will make her feel worse. She needs peace and quiet."

"She is my mother! It is down to me to look after her now."

"She's fine. You go back to London, and if she gets worse, then we'll sort something out."

I was incredulous. I didn't like him much anymore. I had a funny feeling, but I couldn't quite put my finger on it. I just had to organise some home help or a live in carer. At least I knew she would be taken care of.

Several days later, we visited mum's oncologist. I wanted to see what she had to say before taking the plunge and telling mum about the conversation with the radiotherapist.

"Good afternoon, Señora Santiago. Well, Señora Santiago, if you didn't believe in miracles before, you should do now. Your tumor has gone down in size."

"That's good news," said mum. That was weird! The other doctor obviously didn't know what he was talking about because here is mum's specialist saying she is actually getting better, so maybe all my prayers were being answered after all.

"Yes, you're doing really well. Carry on as you are and keep taking the medication. There is no more chemo for you. Just make sure you relax as much as you can and take it easy." I felt so relieved I hadn't told her what the other doctor had said. Things can turn around for the better. What great news!

I left mum with details of a young lady who was coming from an agency. She was going to stay with mum apart from Sundays, when she would go back to her own house as it was her day off.

I left reassured she was going to be safe and well looked after.

Chapter 17

Bon Voyage

Blessed are those who mourn, for they will be comforted.
-Matthew 5:4 NIV

It was the end of September. Liam and I along with the boys were visiting mum for ten days to make sure she was okay. She had finished her radiotherapy and chemotherapy and appeared to be doing very well, and our visits did her the world of good. She loved every minute of them.

At the same time as we were in Spain, my dad was visiting his brother in the south of France, who he hadn't seen in six years. Dad hadn't been on holiday in years when suddenly, completely out of the blue, he decided that he and his best friend Claire were going to go to a seaside resort for a week and have some fun. The decision came as a big surprise to us all, as we had been telling him for ages that he deserved a holiday and how he desperately needed a break. He needed some time away, especially after the amount of stress he had been under lately. He had recently been released from hospital just a few months previously after having recovered from his latest nervous breakdown. This had been brought about by his lodger who'd run up a telephone bill of over £600 in one month. Liam took it upon himself to have a quiet word in the lodger's ear - much to my dad disagreeing with this sort of tactic. Something had to be done; otherwise, he was just going to continue to walk all over my dad, knowing what a soft touch he was and how easily he could be ripped off. The thought of all the bills mounting up had made my dad very unwell. He never had more than a couple of pounds in his pocket at any one time and was worried not knowing how he was going to pay these bills to which the lodger wasn't willing to contribute.

As my dad didn't like confrontation, he had done his best in trying to hold it all in, but all the stress and worry resulted in a stay at the local psychiatric unit. He really needed a change of scenery, but he couldn't see how he could afford it on his disability pension. Liam and I offered to pay for his flight to visit his brother, but then he worked himself up because he was worried about other bills arriving on the doorstep. He got into such a lather, I thought it would be best for him to decide when would be the right time to visit and let him make the decision.

Suddenly, one day dad made an announcement, "I've seen an offer in the paper, and I've booked a week's holiday by the sea with Claire. I've put it on my credit card,"

"Wow, okay, that's fantastic Dad. How exciting! When are you going?" I was so pleased he had actually made a decision.

"In three weeks, half board. It's a great deal and I thought, well you have to do these things, don't you?"

"Good for you Dad. Go Daddy! Go Daddy!" I sang to him encouragingly, having a laugh. While they were away, he and Claire had a great time. He bought himself a nice pair of leather shoes which he also put on his credit card.

One morning shortly after his return, he arrived at my front door like he normally did, for a cup of tea and to bring Oscar and James a small bar of chocolate each. When I opened the door, I could see something wasn't quite right, but I couldn't put my finger on it.

"Hi Dad. How are you?" He pointed to his face and mumbled at me.

"I don't know, I feel a bit funny. I can't talk properly. I keep slurring." I thought he was just being silly. He looked tired which was why I thought he was mumbling. "Talk properly, Dad, move your mouth more."

"I feel fine, but a cup of tea would be nice, please." I wasn't sure whether he was fine or not, but I didn't want to make a big thing of it just in case he started to panic. He was back to his normal self after he had had a cup of tea, as if nothing had happened. Then he made another announcement.

"I've seen some cheap flights to France and I'm going to stay with my brother for a couple of weeks."

"Wow, Dad, you're really pushing the boat out. That's so good. You'll love it. First seaside resorts, now the south of France."

"Well, I put it on my credit card, and I'll pay it back later. Do you like my new shoes? Lovely, aren't they? I'm really chuffed with them." I went over to him and gave him a kiss on the cheek and a big hug.

"Are you ready for another cup of tea Dad?"

It is the little things that make one happy in life. A simple life, being grateful for what you have, even if it's not a lot. There are always people worse off than you.

"So, you're going to be away at the same time as me when I visit Mum."

"Yes, but I don't get back until three days after you," he said.

"Right, so how are you going to get to the airport?"

"My mate Bob said he'll give me a lift. I don't want you running around after me when you have the kids to think about, you have enough on your plate."

"Dad, you know it's not a problem. I can take you."

"It's all sorted now don't you worry about it. Just you look after

Liam and the boys." I agreed with him so as not to stress him.

If he was happy with that, then it was fine by me.

Whilst in Spain, Liam and I celebrated our wedding anniversary. We had a meal in the local restaurant downstairs from where mum lived, and the owner gave us a free bottle of champagne to celebrate the occasion.

We had decided to try for a third baby, hoping for a girl. We had been deliberating whether or not now was the right time, what with mum being poorly. In the end, we decided it would be a good thing. If I became pregnant it would give mum something to look forward to and bring some positivity into her life. It would be an encouragement.

We had a lovely meal it was mum's treat. She enjoyed having us around and the difference in her was apparent. She was so much happier.

We were leaving in the morning to head back to England as Liam had to be back at work. Money had to be earned, bills had to be paid and Oscar was due back at nursery. There was an element of sadness, but mum was ready for a bit of peace and quiet. She had done very well up until now with two young boys in the house. Liam and I spent a lot of time in the park and going for walks with the boys so not to tire her out too much. When we were in the apartment the boys loved playing out on the terrace area. Mum had what seemed like the largest terrace area in the whole of Barcelona. It was the main reason for buying the apartment; because of its size and the great outside space - gold dust in the city.

By the time we arrived back at the apartment and put Oscar and James to bed, Liam and I were very tired. We had to be up early the next day to head to the airport, so we decided to call it a night.

As soon as we arrived back home, I gave dad a call just to let him know we were back safely, and I wanted to know how he was doing. "How's it going Dad? Have you been having fun?"

"Yes, it's been lovely weather here. We've been relaxing, playing cards, but I've been feeling a bit breathless. I don't know why."

"Do you feel alright, Dad? Is everything okay?" I had a feeling everything wasn't okay. "Get Uncle Ian to take you to the doctor for a check-up."

"Yes, I have been like it for a few days now. You know where the toilet is, just outside the living room, well I can hardly walk there, I get there and I'm out of breath."

"Dad, go to the doctor or to the Emergency Department. Please get it checked."

"Yes. Ian has made an appointment for this afternoon. I'll see what they say."

"Okay. Well, I'll phone you back later and you can let me know how you get on. In the meantime, just sit and relax, don't you worry about anything." I always kept a close eye on my father's mental health. I tried my best to make sure he didn't get too worried or stressed about things as I knew what the result could be. I could recognise the early signs of a possible nervous breakdown.

"I will." I was relieved he was going to see a doctor. At least something was getting done. "Is Aunty Carol there? Can I say hello?"

"Carol, it's Evie. She wants to say hello." Dad passed the phone over to my aunt who would be able to give me some more information as to what was going on. Usually, my dad would refuse to see a doctor, claiming there was nothing wrong with him, but he was happy to go along this time.

"Hi, Carol. How's dad doing? He sounds a bit breathless."

"Yes, he's not right. I don't know what's wrong with him, but Ian is taking him to the doctors this afternoon. There's been a couple of times when he has been talking a bit funny, like slurring, and his face has been a bit droopy."

Then it hit me. "Yes, that happened not too long ago, when he came round to visit me. I didn't think it was anything, as he seems to have been fine since. I think he's had a couple of mini-strokes, you know?" I said realizing what was happening, at least he had an appointment with the doctor, they would know what to do.

"Oh my gosh! Do you think so?"

"Yes, it all makes sense now. I will contact dad's doctor and make an emergency appointment for as soon as he gets back. I'll see if they can see him straightaway."

"Yes, he needs to be seen as soon as possible," my aunt agreed.

"I'll phone back later after you get back from the doctors." My heart was beating fast. I had a weird feeling about this, one of my feelings when I know something is about to happen, like a warning sign. There was nothing to do but wait. It was out of my hands.

I finished unpacking the suitcases and put on a load of washing. Liam and I went to the local supermarket to get some milk and fill up the fridge. Dad was on my mind all the time. I kept looking at my watch to see if it was time to call France again. Finally, it was coming up to six o'clock in the evening their time, so they should be back by now.

"Well, how did you get on?" I asked impatiently.

"He reckons my blood pressure is a bit high and he's given me some tablets to thin the blood and other bits and pieces. I don't know what they're all for, otherwise I'm okay. He says to take it easy."

"Do you want me to drive over and bring you back in the car?

199

I'm just thinking of the air pressure in the plane and the altitude. In case it has any effect on your breathing. If you want, I can leave now, and I'll be with you tomorrow evening. We can then have a slow drive back in the car. What do you think? You're due to fly back Wednesday aren't you, the day after tomorrow?"

"Yes, but I'm fine. I don't want you to worry about me, I'll be alright. You're a good girl, Evie, and you have a fantastic family. Liam is very good to you. I know he will always look after you. He loves you very much." Dad was starting to say weird stuff now. He was very calm and knew exactly what he was saying.

"Dad, I'm going to make an appointment for when you get back, so you can see the doctor straight away and have a check-up, just to make sure you are okay."

"Evie, I'm fine. I'll be alright. You have two lovely boys, so look after them."

"Dad, if you change your mind and you want me to come and get you, I will, it's not a problem. Just let me know. I love you, Dad."

"I love you too, my little girl, my little 'tweety pie'." I was holding back the tears which were starting to come from nowhere. Why did I feel that my dad and I were saying goodbye? "I love you, Dad. You know that don't you? Call me if you want anything. Okay?"

"Okay," He said.

"I love you. I'll ring you tomorrow to see how you're feeling."

"Okay, bye bye. God bless."

I put the phone down and sobbed. I thought to myself, why is it the best ones go first? Why did I feel like that was the last time I would ever speak to my dad? It wasn't fair.

"Mummy?" Oscar was looking for me. "I need some help setting up the video in the living room." I wiped away my tears so as not to upset him and went to sort out his video for him.

The next day I was up early. I took Oscar to nursery which he attended three times a week, and James was having his morning nap which he always did after the nursery run. On the way back he would have a snooze which suited me fine, leaving me to get on with the things I needed to do before I had to head back to collect Oscar after his morning of playing and socialising.

It was 9.30 in the morning. I had just sat down at my computer to write a letter to dad's doctor explaining how he was on holiday, and I believed he had suffered what we now thought to be a few mini strokes. I was asking for an urgent appointment ready for when he returned. Then the phone rang. I knew who it was, I knew who it was before I picked up the phone. "Hello Evie, it's Aunty Carol." She sounded sniffly and was noticeably quiet on the phone. I held my breath. It's okay, I said to myself, you knew this was coming.

"Hi Carol, it's a bit early isn't it?" My aunt had never phoned at that time of the day before.

"It's 10.30." She checked her watch.

"Oh yes, 9.30 here." Always remembering France was one hour ahead of the UK.

"Evie, are you sitting down?" she asked. She started to cry.

"Yes, I am."

"Evie love, it's your dad. He's just died." She was now in tears.

"It's okay, Carol. I knew what you were going to say. I knew it last night when I spoke to him. I knew it was the last time I was going to talk to him. I was expecting it. It's okay."

"Now, I don't want you to panic."

"No, no, it's okay." I didn't think I was panicking, but I was unaware my voice was starting to rise, and I was starting to get upset while trying to stay calm at the same time.

"Evie, listen to me. Are you on your own?"

"Yes. Liam's at work, I will call him now. I think he's in a meeting, but I will call him now. It's okay. Don't worry Carol, it's okay."

I had to get to France. I wanted to see my dad before they took him away. I wanted to be with him to say goodbye.

"Listen, where are the boys?" Carol asked.

"Oscar is at nursery and James's asleep."

"I'll call Cindy and I'll get her to come over to be with you."

I asked her. "What happened? Where is he now?"

"He had a pulmonary embolism here in the house. Harry tried to revive him, but he couldn't. The doctor and the ambulance came within minutes, but it was too late. It was so quick, Evie."

"Where is he now?"

"He's in my bedroom. The funeral people are coming soon, I don't know yet what is going to happen. As soon as I know something, I'll call you."

"I'll try and get a flight out as soon as possible. Let me call Liam. I'll call you later."

"Alright, my love. Go make yourself a cup of tea and I'll call Cindy." I sat back down in the chair, tired of pacing up and down the hallway. I knew it, I knew it. I knew this was going to happen. Thankfully, my cousin Cindy lived close by just at the other end of the village.

I phoned Liam's work. "Hi, Lottie, is Liam there please?" I asked in a calm voice.

"Hi Evie, how are you? No, he's in a meeting. Can I get him to call you back?"

"Where is the meeting?"

"He's with David in the City. I'll try and get hold of him for you if you want?"

"Yes, please. Yes! My dad has just died, and I need to go to France. Tell him he needs to come home straight away." The urgency in my voice exploded to slightly rude I would say, but it was urgent.

"I'm so sorry. I'll get him to ring you right away."

"Tell him he needs to come home now! I put the phone down and there was a knock at the door. Carol had managed to phone Cindy, to tell her the news that her uncle had just died, she came over straight away to be with me. I opened the door and burst into tears.

"Right, go and sit down and I'll make you a sweet cup of tea. Have you had a cup of tea yet?" Said Cindy.

"No, I haven't. I need to phone Amanda. She has to collect Oscar for me. She can collect him at the same time as she gets Lilly." I picked up the phone to call Amanda and before I had finished dialing the number, Amanda was knocking at the door. Then the phone rang. It was Liam. Everything now felt okay, now I could speak to him, now I could hear his voice.

"Lottie just told me. I'm on my way home right now. I'm just heading to the train station. Are you on your own?"

"No, I'm fine, Cindy is here, so is Amanda, and I think Aunt Mary is on her way as well. I need to find a flight we need to be with dad. I want to see him before they take him away."

"We'll sort it all out. Don't worry, I'll be home as soon as I can, okay? I love you."

"I love you too." I felt much calmer now I had spoken to Liam. Everything would be alright now he was on the way home.

The organising of the flight was proving difficult. Trying to get there as soon as possible and book a return for the least amount of money was the challenge.

Cindy looked after the boys until Liam's mum and dad arrived. They drove down as quickly as they could, all the way from Shropshire. Thankfully, they were going to stop at our house and look after the boys until we returned, which wasn't going to be for another three to four days at least. Liam drove as fast and as safely as he could all the way to Heathrow, and we parked the car in the first available car park. A couple of hours later we jumped on the Air France flight to Toulouse.

By the time we were sat on the plane, I had a splitting headache, and I didn't think it would be possible for any more tears to fall. I was getting weird looks from the people on the plane as I did look a frightful sight. I hated flying and especially now as we were sat by the wing. "Excuse me, please?" I asked the air hostess. "Do you have another seat available not by the wing? My dad has just died, and I hate flying, I don't like sitting here." She could see the state I was in and told me to wait for a couple of minutes.

"If you'd like to follow me, we have a couple of free seats up in first class."

"Thank you so much." I started to cry again, I couldn't stop.

I couldn't believe my dad was dead. I wished I had a pair of sunglasses to cover my eyes. My eyes were swollen now, and my nose was bright red. This was the first available flight we could get on and it was a two hour drive away from where my aunt lived, but at least we were on our way. My head ached so much, and my mobile hadn't stop ringing with people who wanted to talk to me to make sure I was okay and to give their condolences. This should not be happening.

Hadn't I been told just a few weeks ago while visiting mum's doctor, that she would be lucky if she made it to Christmas? That was one blow, I was preparing myself for my mum to die. What was my dad playing at, popping his clogs before her, without warning? What was going on? As soon as we landed in Toulouse, I called my aunt to tell her we had arrived, she told me the funeral people were there at the house and about to take my dad to the funeral parlour. I would be able to go and visit him first thing tomorrow morning. She asked me what sort of funeral did I want? Had my dad expressed any preference for a burial or cremation? For years he had always insisted that he wanted to be cremated, and to make sure he was not buried. I confirmed it should be a cremation, it was what he wanted.

I was so upset and too exhausted to worry about anything else at this stage. I just wanted some paracetamol, go to bed, and wake up the next day and all of this to have been a bad dream. It was a good thing he was going to be cremated, how else would I have managed to bring him back home? The thought of it made my mind boggle, logistics, coffins in a plane.

The first thing my aunt did when I arrived at her house was to hand me a cup of tea and a couple of paracetamol for the headache. Everyone was in shock and exhausted by the day's events. Harry had gone back to his own house as he was so upset, he was not able to resuscitate his uncle. Dinner had been prepared but not a lot of it was eaten. We sat around the dining room in disbelief and silence. We appreciated how, in hindsight, all the past events had unfolded and how at peace we were about it. It was all good. It was all for the best at the end of the day. He didn't know how poorly mum really was. Had he known she was soon going to die he may have had another nervous breakdown like he did when his own mother died. He had recently been complaining about various little ailments and had only just decided to get them checked out. It wasn't until he had seen his doctor and further appointments had been arranged that he mentioned anything to me. I believe he may have had some form of cancer. Had that been diagnosed he wouldn't have been able to cope. The fact he went on holiday twice for the first time in years and bought himself a new pair of shoes for the first time in a long while was very unusual. There was a plan in place by someone up there and how wonderful for him to pass away in his favourite place, with his brother, whom he admired, in the beautiful sunny south of France. Imagine if it had happened while he was on his own in his little house with no one around him. That would have been awful. Taking everything into consideration it was meant to be, and it happened in the very best way, very quickly, and without any suffering apart for those who were left behind. Realistically you couldn't have asked for a better passing.

Mum was obviously very upset. Although they had been divorced for over thirty years neither of them ever had a proper relationship after that. My dad always joked about them getting back together, but we all knew it was not a good idea, though they did remain good friends. Dad came on holiday with me a couple of times and we stayed with mum, they enjoyed each other's company.

Getting him back to the UK was a bit of a palaver. I stood at the security gates with all the necessary documentation needed when transporting someone's ashes on the plane. I was determined I wouldn't put them through the security X-ray machine, along with the rest of the handbags and coats, as I felt it would be very disrespectful and an awful way to treat my dad. I held them protectively in my arms all the way.

I was not going to put them through to be X-rayed. That's what the letter was for, and anyone could see I was not in the mood to be messed with.

When it was my turn to go through the X-ray machine, I explained to the security man that I was holding my father's ashes. I pleaded with him not to put them through the security machine. The staff were very understanding and sympathetic, they surveyed the letter, and I handed them the urn over the machine. I was so grateful for their understanding. We thanked them and went to sit down by the departure gate. Liam was very protective of me and was ready to sort out anyone who dared to upset me by putting obstacles in our way. As if this whole scenario wasn't upsetting enough. I felt relieved and sat quietly, contemplating what was happening. Suddenly there was a call over the tannoy. "Can Mrs Weaver, please come to the information desk."

"What do they want now?"

"I think I know what it is," said Liam. "I bet it's all your dad's medication in his bag." I had just gathered up all dad's things, clothes and belongings, and just stuck them in his hold-all and was going to sort it all out when we were back home. It was too soon to throw anything away. I had to go back through security to reach the information desk.

"Oh, no, we're going to have to go through it all again. Please don't let them put dad's ashes through, Liam."

"Don't worry. I'll go and explain it all to them." Liam explained to the security guard we had just been called to go back over to the information desk and would it be okay not to put the urn through when we came back as I was already upset over all of this. The man assured him it wouldn't be a problem and to go through. We went to the desk and were asked to follow the lady around to the back of the office where my dad's hold-all had been pulled out.

"Excuse me, Madam, can you identify this bag?" It wasn't her fault; she was just doing her job. My reply was short and sharp.

"Yes, it belongs to my dad."

"And, where is he?" Liam and I looked at each other, and we could see the funny side of what was coming next.

"Right here." I looked down at the small bag with the urn which I was holding tight in my arms. I did feel awful for the lady, but I was so tired. "These are my dad's ashes, he died here on holiday four days ago and now I'm taking them home."

"What about all these medicines in the bag?"

"He'd been poorly, and I haven't thrown anything away yet. Look, here is the letter confirming everything." She had a stunned look on her face and was a bit embarrassed.

"I see, I am sorry for your loss."

"Thank you, I realise now I should have disposed of them beforehand. I'm sorry. Can I go now?" Permission was granted with the understanding that this was a very fraught time. We then headed back towards the security gate and Liam looked for the man who said we could go without putting submitting dad's ashes through the X-ray machine. He was nowhere to be seen, someone else was in his place. Liam was ready to punch someone at this point. We had to go through the whole rigmarole again; this time the ashes did go through the machine.

I held the bag tight throughout the whole flight, and once we had landed, I took the ashes back to dad's house and placed them on the mantelpiece. It wasn't long before I arranged a memorial service for his friends and family who hadn't been able to make it to the funeral service in France. They were able to pay their respects to him here in his home village and attend the interment of his ashes. It was a beautiful service even though I say so myself. I found the best photo I could with my dad wearing the biggest smile. I took it to the local printers to get it enlarged and placed the photo along with his favourite guitar on the altar, with the largest bouquet of flowers I could find, one with the most colours. Harry had said it had to have as many colours as possible because that's how dad was and how he liked to live his life – full of energy and colour.

My friend Joanne looked after the boys while the service took place, and afterwards we all headed to the Social Club where we all had food, drinks and listened to music. There were a few kids there running around, laughing and having fun. My dad would have loved watching them.

Chapter 18

After You've Gone

Even though I walk through the darkest valley, I will fear no evil, for you are with me; your rod and your staff, they comfort me. -Psalm 23:4 NIV

When I returned to the room, mum's breathing had changed. She seemed emotional that her son in law had visited her. The nurses confirmed what was happening. I sat on the bed with my arms either side of her talking to her softly. I was reassuring her everything was going to be alright, and I was here right beside her and how I loved her very much. Mum's cousin was standing by the side of the bed crying, "No, no, no!" Suddenly mum opened her eyes and looked straight at me. In that moment it was just me and her.

"It's okay Mum, it's okay. There is nothing to be afraid of." I said "Dad's waiting for you. I'm here, Mummy, I love you. It's all going to be all okay now." She looked at me peacefully, closed her eyes and she was gone.

The nurse standing beside her bed checked her pulse and confirmed it. He looked bemused, "Wow, if only they all went like that." I didn't quite understand what he meant. "Some of them tend to put up a struggle." He explained. I was pleased she hadn't, I was relieved her passing was just as I had prayed for. It couldn't have been better, a controlled environment, no pain, no struggling, no real suffering, and me by her side, just the two of us. That is how she would have wanted it. My prayers had all been answered, yet again.

"Right, if you would like to leave the room for a few minutes, we will get her ready to go across the road," said the nurse.

"I am sorry, what do you mean? Go where?"

"We'll wash her hair…"

"What? How are you going to do that?"

"We have a special product that washes the hair while it's dry. They will come and get her shortly so you can spend a few minutes before she goes. It won't take long. I will call you in when she's ready."

"Where is she going?"

"To the *tanatorio*, the funeral home across the road. You will have to go over there and take her ID card."

I was reluctant to leave her side, let alone leave the building and go across the road. I thought my mum had just passed away and I was supposed to be bawling my eyes out. I haven't been given a chance. Pedro turned up with his wife - good timing. I didn't remember calling him, or maybe I did. "I have to go across the road and take mum's ID card, so they have all her details."

"Don't worry about that. Why don't you give it to us, and we'll go over for you," suggested Pedro's wife. I thought it was a nice suggestion, which, for some reason, I reluctantly accepted, but I didn't want to leave my mum just yet.

"Thank you, that's very thoughtful of you." I wasn't happy about giving him her private documents, but then again, he was trying to be nice - somehow it didn't feel right.

I leaned against the window at the end of the hallway, oblivious to the people around me, stunned and shocked, the events that had just taken place over the last forty-eight hours going around in my head.

"You can come in now." The nurse held the door open. Okay, here we go. I was scared about this bit. The room I had walked out

211

of just ten minutes ago had changed completely. It was no longer the same room where I had just spent the last twenty-four hours. The sunlight no longer shone through the window, the smiles mum and I had exchanged had gone, and there was no longer any singing. I had sung to her most of the day and throughout the night, all her favourite songs, as I held and kissed her hand. The room was quiet and still, the shutters had been pulled down part of the way, and the lights were turned off. It was as if the sun was hiding behind the clouds. My mum lay peacefully asleep, or so it seemed. I felt she knew we were there, and she was happy and relieved. The oxygen mask and all the tubes and equipment had all disappeared. The room was tidy and clear of clutter. Mum looked presentable, her hair had been washed and groomed and she was no longer struggling to breathe. The stress and lines of pain and discomfort had vanished from her face. She looked younger, she looked happy. Nuria was in the room with me when Pedro returned with his wife and handed me the ID card. For some reason, he wouldn't come into the room where my mum lay.

As I stood at the foot of the bed, I sensed someone was holding my hand, just as I had been holding my mum's all this time. I sensed she had now come over to me and held mine. I felt a love and peace surround me. I knew mum was standing right next to me saying thank you. "Look at my hand," I called to Nuria and Pedro's wife. "Look, someone is holding my hand." They went quiet and looked on. "It's mum, look, she is holding my hand." Pedro's wife backed away a little and said nothing. "I told you she called out my dad's name, didn't I? He was here waiting for her."

"Right, I'm afraid you are going to have to leave now. We are going to take her over the road." A nurse came into the room and told us to say our goodbyes.

"You should be able to see her this evening." She turned to me and gave me a list of instructions. "You will have to bring her clothes as soon as possible so she'll be ready, then go and fill in all the paperwork at administration. You have a couple of hours before they close." The clock was ticking. I had to rush home to choose some nice clothes for her journey. Her nice new shoes and possibly her new blue outfit which she had only bought a couple of weeks ago. "The funeral will probably be tomorrow." She told me. I was having trouble taking it all in. What about all the phone calls I had to make to her friends and relatives? I wouldn't have time to do it all, and what about me? I just wanted to sit down with a cup of tea and reflect on what had happened. I knew things worked fast in Spain when someone dies. They bury their dead the next day, all to do with the heat apparently. Before the funeral, all the friends and family come to say their goodbyes and sit with the body until the time had come for it to be buried or cremated. I wasn't sure how I was going to cope sitting next to a dead person for more than a minute. I had no time to think about it. Liam was back at the flat with the children, where they were happily playing with their toys, or, watching television, without a care in the world, that's just how it should be.

I had never been to the *tanatorio* before and had no idea of what to expect, but if I had expected anything, it would never have been anything like I encountered.

When my English nan died, I remember going to visit her at the back of the funeral home, where she lay in a tiny dark room at the end of a courtyard. It was cramped with hardly any room to move around. If you were hoping to avoid being close to a coffin, you didn't have much luck, as it was immediately in front of you as you walked in. Dealing with that situation hadn't taken long. It was over with very quickly, breathe deeply and go in, give nan a quick kiss on the forehead and run out again. I was taken aback by the coldness of her face. I wondered if being with mum would be similar. I hoped not.

After frantically rummaging around mum's wardrobe, I found the new outfit, a nice blue skirt, a paler blue blouse and matching jacket. I grabbed two pairs of shoes to go with it just in case one of them didn't fit and hurried back to the *tanatorio* before they closed.

Laura, the cleaning lady from work, had just called me and agreed to meet me there so I wouldn't be on my own. I was grateful for the thought. We arrived at the funeral home at the same time. I took a moment before entering and observed the outside of the building. It was a huge, grey, modern-looking building. It reminded me of the NASA space building in Florida but a slightly smaller version. It was distracting, as if the discreet and sombre feeling of death did not fit into this experience. We walked in through the entrance. It was busy with people coming and going through the reception area. We went up a large staircase surrounded by flowers and plants with flowing water cascading either side. The walls and floor were made from beautiful shiny marble. I wasn't expecting that, and it was a pleasant surprise.

In the reception area, to the right, on the wall was a large billboard with numbers from one to twelve running down it. Next to each number was a name. I gave it a quick glance, and I felt as if I had arrived at my local twelve-screen cinema and the notice board was displaying the latest blockbuster films. I didn't take much notice of it to be honest, as it meant nothing to me. I headed to the reception and presented myself to the lady behind the desk. A lady came out and escorted me to a small office and took the bag of clothes from me. Laura decided she was going to get a coffee from the cafeteria located on the first floor and make some calls and left me to get on with it. "I have brought two pairs of shoes, I didn't know which ones would fit best as her feet are very swollen," I said, pointing to the bag.

"Don't worry, they sometimes don't fit so we just tuck them down by their feet or cut the shoes a little. But whatever happens, she will look lovely."

I started to feel dizzy, I was so tired. I felt guilty as I hadn't yet had the time to call anyone to let them know mum had died and here I was, organising her funeral. A man came in and sat down at the desk in front of me. I wondered where the woman had gone and if she was coming back. He started talking.

"Right then, do you have your mum's ID card?" I handed it to him.

"Excuse me, will I be able to see my mum tonight?"

"Yes, maybe, if we get everything sorted beforehand, and if the guys aren't too busy, we will be closing soon." It was getting near to closing time and I wanted to see her before they closed for the night. "Right, the funeral will have to be the day after tomorrow as the chapel is fully booked." He spoke very casually.

"She wants to be buried, she doesn't want to be placed in a wall." I wanted to get that point across before we went any further.

"Oh, I am sorry, there are no burial plots left in the whole of Barcelona."

"She wants to be buried in the ground," I insisted, expecting he could arrange something for me.

"There isn't anything in the city. There are only *nichos* available."

"What do you mean? She doesn't get a choice? She always said she wants to be buried like they do in England, in the ground." I was getting anxious and upset. "Surely there must be somewhere?"

"Well, unless she goes to *Totana.*"

"Where? I have never heard of it."

"It's about forty minutes from here. It's an old park, all ground burials and beautifully manicured gardens."

"So, she can go there?" I wasn't entirely happy with this arrangement. I thought of the times when people go to lay flowers on the graves of their departed, for anniversaries and birthdays. They are usually buried in a cemetery at the end of a village; not having to travel miles away to somewhere they have never heard of. A decision had to be made there and then. There was no time to go away and think about it. This man needed to know right here and now.

"I will just give them a quick call to make sure." He said. I couldn't believe I was having an argument about burying my mum. I thought it would be so simple. I never thought I would have to be so involved.

The man put the phone on hold. "They can fit her in, but they don't have any single plots left. They are all doubles."

"But she only needs a single plot. It is just her!"

"They only have doubles I'm afraid. And yes, it will be more expensive."

"How much more?" He made some calculations on a piece of paper and showed me the figure. "How much?" This wasn't a time to be picky. It was hard to take it all in. Only two hours ago I was sitting on the bed cuddling my mum, and now I was in an office arguing about how much money I was going to have to pay for her funeral.

"Okay, I suppose when my nan dies, which could be sooner rather than later, she could always go in with her." Two for the price of one I thought. That will save on funeral costs for my uncle and judging by how much this was costing I had no other choice.

He put the phone down. "Let's go and choose a coffin." He stood up to leave the office and I started to panic.

"Where are you going?"

"I am taking you next door to choose a coffin for your mother."

"Don't you have a catalogue? I can choose it from a catalogue."

"No, they are all next door, you have to come next door."

I had a phobia of coffins, ever since my mum's aunt died when I was thirteen and my mum took me to see her. I had nightmares for years after where I was trying to get as far away from coffins as I could. I didn't like them. Organising my dad's funeral had been so much easier in comparison. Even in choosing the coffin, there had only been a choice of two and they were printed nicely in a little booklet, no problem.

I stood up to follow the man as I could sense he was getting annoyed and impatient with me. It was literally the room next door. I stopped in my tracks when he opened the door. The room was full of coffins, wall to wall, floor to ceiling. I had never imagined anything like it. I held on to Laura's arm, who had been waiting outside the office for me, and stood there for a couple of minutes, unable to enter the room. The man was looking at his watch and urged me to come in and to get a bloody move on. He probably wanted to get home before the rush-hour traffic. Laura at this point, was dragging me in by the arm, but I was still resisting. For them, it was the most natural thing. What was the problem? It was just a room with about fifty coffins for you to choose from, all different colours and made from different materials and types of wood. Eventually, I had to face it. I held on tight to Laura, squeezing her arm, and repeatedly telling myself, "it's okay." He pointed out different types and at different prices, some expensive and elaborate and others more modest. I picked one out and left the room faster than I entered.

After about an hour of sorting out paperwork, bills and payments, my mum was ready. We were directed upstairs and told she was in room number nine. Her name was now on the big board at the entrance. The board advertised which room the deceased was in. At the top of the stairs was a beautiful atrium. It was an ample open space with a massive water feature in the centre and palm trees scattered around.

Surrounding the garden were the various rooms, with a notice outside each one stating the name of the deceased so friends and relatives could find their loved ones easily.

I found the room where my mum was and stood outside, not wanting to go in for fear of what I was going to have to face, but at the same time desperate to be with her until the time came for the funeral. I didn't want to leave her on her own. I hesitated, but then finally remembering this was my mum we were talking about, why would I be scared of being with her? I felt a peace within me. I knew it would be okay and there was no need to be afraid. I found the strength to go in. I opened the door very slowly and found an empty room with a table and a couple of chairs and a small leather sofa. Some pictures hung on the wall, and there was a kettle for making tea and coffee on a table in the corner and a toilet should you need one. Mum was nowhere to be seen. In another corner was a closed door.

I had no idea what was behind it, so I opened it very slowly and peered into the room. There, in the middle of the room, was my mum lying in a coffin which was glass-encased. I gave out a little laugh and shed a tear. The room was large enough so one could move comfortably around the coffin, and was well lit. My mum looked beautiful. Someone had done her make-up and had given her a manicure and her nails were nicely polished. Her brand-new shoes lay by her feet and she had a slight smile on her face, which was nice to see, but at the same time made you wonder what she was smiling at. She looked so peaceful, and I found it funny as she reminded me of Snow White and the Seven Dwarfs - when Snow White is lying in her glass coffin, waiting for Prince Charming to come along. You could see the funny side of it. It was the first time I didn't have to run to anywhere, I could just stand still for a few moments and be allowed to cry. I cried and caressed the glass as if I were stroking my mum. The whole place looked lovely and there was a tranquillity about it. It amazed me how natural everything was and how very matter of fact it was. No one was bawling their eyes out, and there didn't seem to be a sombre mood in the air as is usual when someone dies. It was all very natural.

I only had twenty minutes left to spend with her before I was asked to leave and told I could come back tomorrow morning when they reopened at 9.30. It was now coming up to nine o'clock at night.

When I arrived back at the flat I had so many phone calls to make. Liam made me a cup of tea and I sat down to ring round all those who I thought were the most important and needed to know first. I picked up the phone and as I went to speak to the person on the other end of the receiver, nothing came out. My mouth was moving but no words came out. I just couldn't do any more. I passed the phone to Liam and left him to speak to the person on the other end. I hadn't stopped talking and singing to my mum for the past couple of days, and trying to arrange things, I was exhausted.

The following day's events seemed surreal. I had to break into the safe hidden in mum's cupboard, where she kept all her legal documents and paperwork for the apartments, hoping there was an insurance policy that would cover the funeral costs. Liam and I certainly didn't have £2,000 to pay for everything and I was sure there had to be some kind of document that would cover it all, but there wasn't. The arranged appointment with the solicitors came and went as my mum had died before she could sign any paperwork. I had a lot of explaining to do. I was sure Pedro would understand the situation and do the right and honourable thing and grant mum's last wishes. Surely, he would understand.

The funeral itself was an intimate affair with a small gathering of family, a couple of friends and a few people from the neighbourhood. Mum didn't have many friends, but she did know a lot of people. My mum's brother and his family came, and I was pleasantly surprised that Simon, my former boyfriend had taken the time to fly over from England, to pay his respects and to support me and Liam. Although we were no longer together, we remained good friends. Even my cousin Daniel and his new wife, drove from their house (which was close to the French - Spanish border) just for the day so that they could look after the boys for me, while I attended the funeral. I was touched by such a deep show of love and support from so many of my family and friends. I felt truly blessed!

The day after the funeral, I arranged for Pedro to come and meet me and Liam for a coffee, so I could discuss the situation with him. He came with his wife, and we sat downstairs in the bar with a couple of coffees and a bottle of water. I couldn't understand his coldness towards me. I thought he might take me under his wing and look after me as a favour to my mum, whom he admired and loved so much. I explained what had happened and how mum had arranged a meeting with the solicitor, and I thought he would agree and revert everything back as mum had wanted. His wife didn't look me at me once. She avoided all eye contact, and she didn't speak a word to me. It seemed as if she wasn't allowed to. "Oh, I have such a headache. I am going to ask for some more water and take some paracetamol." That was all she said. She was so nervous for some reason and wouldn't stop fidgeting. I on the other hand, was feeling very calm.

"You have to wait for the reading of the will, which isn't done until one month after the person has died," Pedro said.

"Yes, I know that, but are you prepared to do as mum wished?"

"I won't know anything until the will has been read. We will have to see what it says in a month's time."

"I know what it says. I just told you." Why wasn't he listening?

"Until a month passes, we can't do anything. Oh, look at the time, we have to go," Pedro said as stood up to leave.

"Oh? Okay then. If I have any problems, I will give you a call then," I said, unsure of what was panning out here.

Something didn't feel right. Why was he in such a hurry? I had known this guy for nearly ten years.

I was baffled. All I could do was sit in mum's apartment, wait, and run the business. I kept the business running because I wasn't sure what else to do. The supervisor was very capable of running it without any problems, I thought of all the girls who were relying on the place being open to earn some money. The best I could do was to leave everything as it was for the moment. It was a part of mum and I wanted it to carry on for the time being.

My mother-in-law flew in the next day to spend some time with me while I hung around deciding on what should be my next step. Liam returned to England and back to work but felt happy knowing he was leaving me in the company of his mum. My mother-in-law and

I got on very well together and it was always a pleasure to have her around. I toyed with the idea of going back to England, but there had been so many robberies recently in the flats, I really didn't want to leave mum's unattended, especially with all her valuables in there. As soon as I had a copy of the will in my hand, I would head back to England. I was going to make sure I was going to be the first one to receive the copy of the will and have it read by the solicitor.

I had tried to contact the *gestor* with whom my mum had spoken, since I had been informed that without her signature, everything would stay as it was. I was stupid if I thought Pedro was going to do a good deed and hand over the entirety of his newfound estate, which was a handsome sum. For some reason, the *gestor* never seemed to be available. I had walked over to his office on a few occasions and finally, after having sat outside for forty-five minutes, a man walked up off the street and was heading into the offices. "Hello, are you Señor Jimenez?"

"Yes."

"I'm Mrs Santiago's daughter, I have been trying to get hold of you for a few days now and you haven't returned any of my calls."

"Come in." He reluctantly showed me into his office and did everything to avoid the matter in hand.

"I have a big problem," I said. "I need you to sign a paper confirming my mum called you and had arranged to change her will. I have explained it to the other guy and for some reason, he is ignoring me."

"Oh, I am so sorry, I have no recollection of the call."

"Sorry, what? Yes, you do! I spoke to you myself! Of course you must have a recollection of the call."

"No, I don't, I don't know anything about it."

Something was seriously wrong here. I thought I was going to throw up. I wasn't going to stand for this. Something started to rise in me.

"Of course you do! What about the will you would have had drafted ready for my mum to sign! You'll have it in your files somewhere!" I had to explain that bit again to him. "You are a *gestor*. You're supposed to keep all your notes. Where is the paperwork you should have prepared ready for the appointment with my mum at our house?"

"I have nothing!" he said, getting extremely flustered. "I threw it all away so there were no remains of any evidence!" I paused in shock for a second, and then I went for him.

"What do you mean you threw it away so there was no evidence? Evidence of what? Who are you to be throwing so-called evidence away? You should be keeping stuff, surely? For what reason would you throw anything away?" Our voices were starting to rise and people outside the office were looking on with concerned looks on their faces.

"Look, I have no records of this, and you really need to go now." And with that, he stood up and ushered me out. I was too flabbergasted to argue. He had said his piece and none of it added up... Or did it?

Back at the apartment, the boys were restless and bored with being cooped up in the flat. They were used to being outside in the garden running up and down, with a larger variety of toys to play with. There wasn't much point in my staying in Barcelona. I may as well go back home and return three and a half weeks later, ready to collect the will and see what I could do then.

I was still concerned about my mum's belongings, so I decided to take the most valuable stuff with me for safety. Up until then, every

223

apartment in my mum's block had been burgled. Even during the day, people had broken into the homes while the residents were in their beds having a siesta. No one had tried to enter mum's apartment because of the dogs, they would bark at the slightest noise. They wouldn't have stood a chance, thank goodness, but with no dogs and the house empty that would be a different story. I wasn't going to take the chance.

My mother-in-law and I found a couple of cardboard boxes and began to carefully wrap the beloved ornaments and precious stones which mum had collected and loved so much. Fabian, a friend of mine who lived on the other side of town, came to give us a hand to pack and to say goodbye as we were heading off the following morning. I had planned to drive back to England in my mum's car as we had too much stuff to carry on a plane, together with two small boys. It made sense to borrow her car, which I drove more than she did anyway. She didn't like going too far, preferring to go everywhere by taxi, as it was much easier when it came to traffic and parking in and around the city.

As we selected the most essential items and wrapped them in newspaper, Fabian and I just stood there surrounded by newspaper and boxes and burst out laughing at how surreal this whole situation was. We started to laugh at what was happening, then we cried with laughter, hysteria was setting in. How is it you can laugh so much in times of tragedy? We couldn't fit a single thing more in the car. The boot was full to the brim. I thought of taking some of her beautiful clothes and jackets and giving them away to a charity shop back home, all of them were from top designers and a lot of them brand new. I gathered up the collection of perfumes with the hope of taking them with me, so every time I smelt them, I would be reminded of her. I left the boys' pushchairs, toys, bikes and videos behind and loads of other bits because I knew I would be returning very soon. I would collect the children's things and would calmly go through my granddad's possessions then. I wanted to take his sword from when he was in the army and his pictures. I'd be more relaxed when I returned.

We drove through France listening to "The Best of the Rat Pack" and classic old songs. My mother-in-law enjoyed that sort of music, so did I. Every so often a song would come on and I would start to cry, "Mum loved this one…" or "This was my dad's favourite…" and then start crying all over again.

It had only been a few days since we returned and I was settling back into my English way of life, I had not long put the kids to bed when the phone rang, it was the night-time supervisor.

"Hi, Evie, we had a visit today from the police, they were asking some weird questions. I don't know if you know anything about it?"

"No." Came my bemused reply.

"Well, I thought I would ask because I know your mum had a policeman friend, so I was wondering if you could have a word with him and see if he knew anything about it."

"Yes, good idea. I'll give him a ring right away and I'll call you later." That was strange. Why would we have a visit from the police out of the blue? They all knew us around there. I picked up the phone to make the call to Pedro to see if he could shed any light on the case. "Hi, Pedro, am I calling at a bad time? Can you talk?"

"Yes, what is it?"

"I have just had a call from the supervisor saying there was a visit from the police this morning, asking some questions about who owned the place, and I don't know what they wanted. Do you know anything about it?"

"Why, where are you at the moment?" He seemed to be ignoring my question.

"I'm in England. Why? I thought I would come home while I wait for the reading of the will."

"I already have the will and she has left everything to me."

"What do you mean you already have the will? It's not supposed to be available until a month has passed."

"My solicitor got it for me. You can ask your solicitor to get it for you. Get yourself a solicitor."

"I already have one."

"Then you should ask him to get it for you." My body went cold, and the world seemed to stop for a moment, and suddenly it hit me. I had been done. It was all a ploy. He wasn't playing Mr Nice Guy; he never had been. All the pieces of the jigsaw seemed to fit; the penny dropped. Oh, my God. My mum had been swindled. We had been set up.

"Where is your mum's car now?" Oh no! was I going to be in trouble now?

"What car?" Okay, I can play this game too.

"Your mum's car. Where is it?"

"It's in the garage, isn't it? The last time I saw it, it was in the garage." Like him, I decided to try and divert his attention. "So, have you thought about our conversation in the bar?"

"All I know is, everything has been left to me. Get a solicitor and get your own copy of the will."

"Yes, I'll do that. Thank you for your help. Anyway, I had better go. I'll give you a ring soon." I changed my tone and played it cool, knowing I had an emergency on my hands again. If he had the will, he would now have the right to go into the flat and take all mum's stuff. I knew I had to get there before him. Once again, I was a bag of nerves on a mission. I called the supervisor back.

"Hi, it's me. Listen carefully, I want you to send all the girls home now, right away, and lock the place up nice and tight. Keep the keys until I get there. I'll give you a ring as soon as I arrive."

I didn't want there to be trouble of any kind for the girls at work. Now things had changed, and it was possible we may no longer have the support from the local police as we did before, anything could happen. I needed to play it safe.

I ran into the living room to tell Liam what was going on. The time now was ten o'clock at night. He knew as well as I did what we had to do. Looking back, it was insane. I grabbed a couple of bags and we gently put the boys in the car trying very hard not to wake them and sped off into the night. We had to get to the flat before Pedro did.

Now he knew I was abroad he could make the most of the situation. I would never get into the apartment again. I was happy with the fact that he would have a large bill from the locksmith after having tried to get into every room. Because mum lived on her own and because of the burglaries she had a lock put on every door for every room, so when she went out and if the worst came to the worst, the robbers would have a hard job of getting beyond the front door.

When I left, I locked each room with the key and carried the keys with me, so that would take up some time. I phoned Enrique, asking him to go to the flat in the morning to remove as much as he could of the boy's belongings, the perfumes, and any papers he might find, in case I needed them at a later date.

Enrique managed to park not far from the front of the building, but as he was about to get out of the car, he saw Pedro and a locksmith approaching. He promptly got back in his car and laid low.

I never got to say goodbye to my mum's place. The neighbours saw all her belongings and my bits and pieces in the bin, photos, toys and my granddad's sword which I had wanted to give to my uncle. Everything was thrown out as if it were rubbish.

I had left the flat with every intention of going back to lovingly sort through mum's things, it is part of the grieving process, but no, nothing. For months afterwards, the boys asked for certain toys and their bikes which they knew were left at Yaya's house for them to play with.

"Mummy, can you ask the man for our toys back?" Oscar was desperate to play on his Spiderman motorbike which his nan had bought him for Christmas. I couldn't tell them they had been thrown away. How could I explain to my four year old son why he would never see his nan again, or his toys, or what we were about to go through. I would have to wait and tell him when he was old enough to understand. Sometimes I find it hard to understand myself.

Chapter 19

Court Hearings

For I know the plans I have for you," declares the LORD,
"plans to prosper you and not to harm you,
plans to give you hope and a future.
-Jeremiah 29:11 NIV

As soon as I put the phone down from speaking with Pedro, it hit me. Had this been his plan all along? Over the last year or so, had he been brainwashing my mother, encouraging her to disinherit me so he would get the whole of her estate?

Liam and I gently took the boys out of their warm toasty beds and put them in the car carefully wrapped up in their duvets and with their pillows, making sure we didn't leave Travelling Ted behind. Oscar had a big cream teddy bear which was as tall as him, and for some reason whenever we went on holiday in the car the bear had to come too, so we ended up calling him Travelling Ted. Over the years Travelling Ted's tummy became thinner and thinner as a result of being slept on and cuddled up to, as Oscar liked to use it as a pillow.

Liam drove as fast and as safely as he could. Thankfully, Dover was just a ninety-minute drive away from our house, making it easily accessible for occasions like this. We boarded the first ferry heading towards Calais, the smell of ferry fuel hanging in the air. We squinted as the bright lights of the car deck assaulted our eyes and adjusted from the comfortable soft night-time lights outside. There were bangs and clanging as cars were directed to their respective secure positions. The boys woke up with surprised looks on their faces to find themselves boarding a ferry, but then proceeded to be full of energy and excitement as we headed up the stairs to the passenger decks and the soft play area. They were the only children on board. It was one o'clock in the morning. Liam went in search of coffee for us and drinks for the children while I sat, bemused, and tired, watching the boys happily play.

After disembarking from the ferry, we were ready to continue our journey south. We drove through the night. Our hearts were heavy with worry, my brain going twenty to the dozen; questioning, wondering, exclaiming to myself, "How could this be happening? Why was this happening? How did I not see this before? How stupid was I?"

Daylight crept up over the horizon. I always enjoy watching the sun rise after having driven all night. There is something magical about it. With each new day comes new beginnings and opportunities. Liam did all the driving, bless him, he had done an excellent job, with the kids fast asleep in the back. I couldn't sleep for worrying and my heart was pounding. This was now a race, and I prayed Enrique would get to the flat in time to get some of the children's things out at least. Now Pedro knew we weren't in the country there was nothing to stop him entering the house, changing all the locks, and claiming his alleged inheritance. All this time he would have assumed I was in the flat waiting for the thirty days to be up so that we could have the reading of mum's last will and testament, which we now knew was already in his possession. There was no one to stop him. I had given him the perfect opportunity to take a part of my life and trample all over it.

The purpose of waiting thirty days is to give the family members time to grieve, then receive their inheritance without getting too upset or angry should they not be in agreement with what they had inherited - or not as the case may be: that's what my solicitor told me anyway.

I thought he would take everything from the flat, but as it turned out, he didn't take anything; he just threw it all out into the rubbish containers outside, which to me was worse. None of it was of any value to him, no emotional value.

Enrique had gone there first thing in the morning as I had requested. Just as he pulled up in his car, he saw them approaching the apartment, Pedro and a locksmith carrying a small bag of tools.

Poor Enrique, he would have been so nervous. This had nothing to do with him, he was out of his depth, but because he liked my mum and she had always given him work when he needed it, he was happy to take the risk. He was the only one with a spare key to the flat anyway so I couldn't have asked anyone else. As soon as he saw them coming, he hid and once he saw them enter the building, he turned his car around and headed home. He knew challenging them was out of the question, there was nothing more we could do. It was over.

I was never going to see the boys' stuff again or mum's family photos. I wasn't going to be able to clear the flat, say goodbye, no real closure.

We hadn't long arrived at my aunt and uncle's house near Perpignan, in France, (where we intended to rest for a while) when Enrique phoned my mobile apologising for not being able to complete the task. We planned to leave the boys with my aunt and uncle for the day while Liam continued to drive me to Barcelona. I reassured Enrique it was okay, I totally understood. I was grateful he had even tried.

Liam and I still had another three and a half hours drive before reaching Barcelona, but the race was now over. He had the upper hand.

At least we could stop for a moment and rest. We were all so happy and relieved to see my aunt and uncle, especially the boys. They saw them as grandparents, and they were treated like grandchildren. It was so lovely to be with them, in their house, in a safe environment. It was familiar and homely, we felt safe and loved.

That afternoon I made some phone calls. I had to find legal representation and quick. I had to contest my mother's will, if not for me but for her. I needed a solicitor as soon as possible. A friend recommended one and I arranged an appointment to see him the next day in Barcelona. I explained the urgency of the matter and how I lived in England, not Spain, and had to go back as soon as I could. Liam still had a business to run, and the boys needed a routine.

The next morning Liam and I set off in the car once more, leaving the boys behind laughing and having fun, making paper swords and shields with their great uncle, and chasing him around the garden, wielding their swords at him. No doubt they would be spoilt with a trip to the beach and ice cream later.

I met with Señor Ignacio, who was going to be my solicitor. I had tried calling my mum's solicitor, Señor Garcia, whom I had dealt with in the past. The very man my mum had trusted so much and said to go to if ever I was in trouble. But he was unable to help me as he was representing Pedro - the person I was making a claim against. Well, it made sense really; it was Pedro who had recommended Señor Garcia to mum in the first place.

Come to think about it, the four million pesetas bail money I paid the court to get mum out of prison, Señor Garcia had kept it all as his fee for apparently getting her released. There had been no evidence and no charge, so she was going to come out sooner or later anyway. I preferred sooner, so the bail was paid. I ask myself, could the entire episode have been a set up between Pedro and Señor Garcia? Had they split the bail money between the two of them?

Señor Ignacio agreed to help me contest the will and - with a lot of luck – maybe get it revoked, back to mum's original wishes which she expressed before she died, but he wasn't making any promises. At least we had *"La Legitima"* to fall back on.

Thankfully in Spain, the law prohibits anyone to completely disinherit their "legal beneficiaries" – their immediate family, their spouse or, as in my case, their children. There is a protective law called *"La Legitima"*. With this law you are entitled to a minimum of twenty-five per cent of whatever the estate is worth. However, if the person who wants to write you out of their will can give a good enough reason in the eyes of the law as to why you shouldn't receive anything, then you could lose everything.

The only way you can be denied *"La Legitima"* is if the person disinheriting you can prove you abused or neglected them or denied them food. Another reason would be, they were physically or morally mistreated, which obviously I had never done any of these things.

Señor Ignacio seemed a nice enough man who had recently taken over the running of his father's firm. Whether he anticipated the seriousness and the possible corruption that was going on, I do not know. For all I knew he could have been part of it himself. I had no choice but to trust him. He was the only hope I had in this whole situation. He set the ball rolling by sending a citation to Pedro and his solicitor. I wrote a fifteen-page document with a blow-by-blow account of conversations, comments made, and statements. He was impressed by the amount of detail I had included and asked if I had ever thought of taking up law as a career. I just wanted to make sure no stone was left unturned. It was a true account of what happened, a complete timeline, the sequence of events as they happened all the way back to Oscar's birthday party. My case all laid out on a Word document.

Señor Ignacio sent me to get certain certificates from another part of the city, but I had to wait until the next day before I could collect them. Liam headed back to France to be with the boys, and I stayed with my friend Fabian in his flat, he had a spare room where I could stay. At least I knew I would be safe there. Everywhere I went, I kept looking over my shoulder to make sure no one was following me. Based on past experiences, I wasn't being paranoid, just careful and alert. We see things happen in films and think it's all made up and it doesn't happen in real life, but it does! I even went to the British Consulate asking for help and advice and tried to explain what had happened, but the lady behind the desk didn't want to believe there could possibly be any corrupt policemen or solicitors out there who would do such a thing. It was a real case of who can you trust? I was turned away by the very people I thought may be able to help me. It felt as if I was in an American spy film. Unfortunately, there was no superhero anywhere to be seen.

Fabian had the tiniest of flats right in the centre of Barcelona, on the fifth floor, with no lift. It was an old building. The living room only had room for a small sofa with a table in front of it. The television sat on a wall cabinet. There was hardly any room to walk around. There were only two bedrooms, or should I say one and a half bedrooms. The half bedroom was part of the hallway which had been partitioned off. I felt safe knowing no one knew where I was.

A feeling of peace enveloped me, and I felt a presence reassuring me everything was going to be okay. The way I saw it I had two choices: I could be angry and scream and have a nervous breakdown, or I could just trust in the peace I felt. I didn't feel any anger towards Pedro whatsoever, I don't think I had the energy to be angry, but something was driving me forward. I didn't quite understand what or where it was coming from. Was it God? Was he speaking to me through this? There was a warmth and confidence about it, a shielding. I felt an inner voice saying, "It's okay, trust Me," then saying, "You don't need that money anyway, it's dirty money. I am going to provide for you. Trust in Me; I've got this." That night I slept like a log; it was the best night's sleep I had had in a long time.

The next day after sorting, collecting, and signing certificates and documents, and authorising the solicitor to represent me, there was nothing more to do but wait. It could take anywhere between four to six months just to receive a date for the court hearing - which might then be set in another six or eight months later. I booked the first available flight back home. The earliest flight was leaving late afternoon heading for Luton. I was longing for some normality.

Very early that same day in France, Liam had strapped the boys into the car, loaded up with their favourite DVDs for them to watch on the long journey back to England. They were surrounded by games and Liam had a pile of children's CDs to hand ready to insert on demand into the car stereo. They were always so well behaved. Liam would stop every so often so they could go for a pee, have lunch and stretch their legs. If there was a play park, they were encouraged to run around and play on the swings or slide. They never complained.

When the plane touched down at Luton airport, my friend Amanda was there waiting for me. It was getting late, about 8.30 or nine o'clock in the evening. I didn't talk too much on the car journey home as I really didn't want to relive the past few days, so Amanda filled me in on what had been happening at home while I had been away. As Amanda's car approached the turn into our road, we saw Liam turn in just before us, coming from the opposite direction. He was arriving at the same time. He had left the south of France earlier the same day, I left Spain that afternoon, and we both arrived at our house in England at the same time. It was quite comical. What were the chances of that?

The weeks went slowly by, and we carried on with our lives and sometimes my mind would wander off wondering how all of this would end. Would the judge look favourably on me and say yes to revoking the whole will, as my mum had so desperately wanted? I asked myself if I had done enough to prove my case. It was not a case of me *trying* to prove my right to the inheritance - because it *was* my right. The case for me was about the conversation mum had with her *gestor*, Señor Jimenez, instructing him to reinstate me as the sole, universal heir; then him denying ever having the conversation. I may have a very good case if he showed the judge the copy of the will that was waiting to be signed. I found it hard to believe the situation I was in. You couldn't make it up. If it did get revoked, our lives would change financially, if it didn't, then I suppose our lives would carry on as before. It felt like everything was going to be taken away from me and that all the odds were stacked against me. I had to handle all of this alone, I had no idea what I was doing. Liam didn't speak any Spanish, and Spanish law is a minefield, especially when it comes to contesting wills. Liam was very good at administration and financial matters, I always trusted him to deal with everything, he always did a good job. On this occasion, he was rendered redundant. All he could do was look after the boys and be there to hold me when I came home.

A couple of months went by when I received a counter-claim copy from Pedro's lawyer, stating that not only had I been disinherited with everything being left to Pedro, (something I already knew) but also explaining how I wasn't entitled to *"La Legitima"* in any shape or form.

Señor Ignacio had tried to reassure me from the beginning if the worst came to worst and we didn't manage to get the will revoked it would be very difficult for me not to be entitled to *"La Legitima"*, so at least I had something to fall back on. I lived in hope.

Señor Garcia, Pedro's solicitor, stated in the document the reasons preventing me from being entitled to *"La Legitima"*.

The first reason was that I had kept my mum locked in the attic whilst she visited us in England, without any food or heating whatsoever. Well, that was a blatant lie to start with! I contacted Señor Ignacio immediately explaining how Liam had converted the loft, especially for her. He spent ages installing the best loft insulation and boarding out the entire loft space. We bought two oil-filled radiators, a couple of lamps and bedside tables from the large furniture shop in the city, to decorate the room so she would feel at home. Not forgetting a selection of rugs to go either side of the lovely double bed. We wanted to create a space she could call her own and she could come over as often as she liked.

Another reason why I apparently wasn't entitled to anything, was because Liam and I had stuffed my mum into the boot of the car, driven to a field somewhere in the snowy countryside far away, and apparently dumped her there!

I was raging and laughing at the same time at how ridiculous it all sounded. I searched for a weather forecasting website and somehow managed to find all the historical weather reports for the day and week this was all supposed to have happened. All the information confirmed it was spring, it was sunny. There hadn't been any snow anywhere in the UK or Europe in the entire month. That was the only evidence I could find to defend myself from the lies said against me.

These claims and accusations were ridiculous and heart breaking. It was awful. I was so angry at my mum for even suggesting such a thing. How could she have come up with something like that? I knew if she were alive now, she would have been so regretful and upset at what she had done and the things she had said. I was more upset for her. It was all in the hands of the judge now and I just prayed that he or she would be a nice judge and not one who may have been coerced by Pedro's people.

Finally, the court date came through, yet again, we headed south to Spain.

As we all gathered and waited to go into the court building, I saw him. It was the first time I had seen Pedro since that morning in the bar. My heart started to beat faster, and I became anxious. I couldn't bear to even look at him. A wave of anger from deep inside me seemed to creep to the surface from where it had been simmering or sleeping. I didn't want to be anywhere near him. Seeing him now, and realising what I now knew, made me feel both sad and angry for my mum. A multitude of emotions were running through me at this point. Had she been aware of what was going on, she would have been in an uncontrollable rage. She would have sought revenge, stopping at nothing and be happy to pay the price for it.

The court hearing was going to be all in Spanish, so my solicitor, Señor Ignacio, kindly arranged for an interpreter to sit with Liam during the hearing so he could understand what was being said. Although, he wouldn't be able to take part or say anything, he would have someone to sit with him, and Liam would be praying for me. I had asked Laura, my mum's cleaning lady, to be a witness for me. After all she had seen me recently, looking after mum every other week, running the business, travelling back and forth over the last year and a bit. She had known me for a couple of years, and I was sure she would vouch for me. She said she would, but on the day of the court hearing Señor Ignacio told me he had received a call from her saying she wasn't coming. Had someone been in contact with her and advised her not to come? Did she feel intimidated and scared?

Thankfully, Fabian was going to be a witness for me as he had been a good friend for many years. He was my only witness, I just had him to back me up. My other three witnesses had decided they had something more important to do than appear in court for me. No one was going to intimidate Fabian, he had nothing to lose. He knew mum well; he knew me and knew everything that had been going on.

We walked into an empty courtroom. It was the first time I had ever been in a court building, so I had nothing to compare it with, only from films or the television. At the top of the room was a long table with several seats, where the solicitors would sit at either end, and in the centre the judge and his assistants. Everyone else sat facing them. There was seating for no more than a hundred people in the room. I was extremely nervous, and I had no idea what to expect. I needed a drink and I wanted to turn around and go home.

We all settled ourselves in the designated areas, me at the front on my own, Liam further back and Fabian sitting not too far behind me. A few minutes later someone announced the judge was coming in and we should all stand up. I wondered if, at some point, a group of policemen would tackle me to the ground and take me to a cell somewhere in a basement if I said something wrong - like they sometimes do in the films. I desperately wanted Liam to be able to sit next to me and hold my hand.

Three people in black gowns walked in together, two men and a lady. On seeing the two men I thought, 'that's it, I'm done for.' A male judge is obviously going to side with Pedro, and I will leave here with nothing. I wondered if the younger-looking lady judge was just learning the ropes, and what she might think of this case. I didn't know what role any of them played or even why there were three of them. We waited until they were seated before we could take our seats again.

The lady with the black gown sat in the middle and began to speak. It was her; she was the judge, and she oversaw the handling of this case. She looked late thirties–early forties and had a friendly look about her. I felt somewhat happier and reassured.

Pedro was called up first and stood in front of the judges, legs slightly apart, his arms behind his back, with his back facing me. Before anyone had spoken to him or addressed him, he started speaking. "Your Honour, I have no idea why I'm here. This is ridiculous. This case is a complete waste of time. I am the legal and final heir of this estate, and this is just wasting our time, your Honour. I shouldn't be here. You know who I am, you know how upstanding I am, I just wanted to say this is absolutely ridiculous and we shouldn't be here."

I was astounded. How could he speak to this lady like that? I thought you were only allowed to speak when you were spoken to. I understood that you should only make a comment when asked for your opinion. Before she had introduced herself, here he was trying to take advantage of his position, "I don't know why we're here, what are we doing here? You know who I am. Let us all go home."

I prayed to God to keep me calm, just keep me calm. I needed to be calm and not lose the plot right now. I was hanging on by a thread. Pedro sat down after what seemed to be a short time. My solicitor asked him just a couple of questions: what was his name and what was his position? He didn't ask anything about the conversations I had with him, about me trying to come over and look after my mum. No questioning at all.

Now it was my turn. I made sure I was extra polite and very English. "Yes, Your Honour. No, Your Honour." I was as respectful and patient as I could be, slightly bowing my head with reverence to this person who commanded respect. Hopefully, she would be able to see straight through Pedro and believe in me, and how incapable I was of doing the things alleged against me.

The judge asked me various questions and I answered them in full. She asked about the argument I had with my mum right at the beginning, the one that had brought all this about in the first place. So, I explained everything that happened, word for word. I explained how Cindy had arrived after her friend's funeral to Oscar's birthday party, and that mum and she had never seen eye to eye. But as I very calmly started to tell her my side of the story, a floodgate of tears burst forth. It was as if I was reliving it all once more, but now I was full of sadness and disbelief at my mother's complete overreaction and total misunderstanding of the situation. My mouth was so dry with nerves I had to stop. "Please, could I have a glass of water? My mouth is so dry." I could barely speak.

"Can somebody get this lady a glass of water please?" I could see compassion in her face, and I felt she knew I was telling the truth. She

241

knew there was something not quite right in this scenario. She then proceeded to ask me about the four million pesetas I had stolen from my mum. My mouth dropped open in shock. I had no idea what she was talking about. What four million pesetas? This, again, was a lie constructed to stand against me. She could see from the look on my face I had no idea what she was talking about.

I was desperate for her to ask me about the initial conversation with Señor Jimenez, mum's *gestor,* and mum's instructions for changing the will and the follow up discussion when he told me he had destroyed all the evidence. I wanted to say, "why are you not speaking to Señor Jimenez and asking for the notes that he would have made at the time?" Why were we not asking for the draft Mum had asked to be drawn up ready for signing? Where was it? Why was nobody looking into this? Apparently, that didn't matter, it had nothing to do with this case. I couldn't tell her how to do her job. I wasn't allowed to mention things that weren't being asked of me. I found it all very frustrating.

After a couple of hours, it was all over. I waited outside for Señor Ignacio to see what was going to happen next. When would she give her verdict? Señor Ignacio informed me they were going to call Señor Jimenez, the *gestor* to come to court so he could share his side of things, but it wasn't going to be today. It was going to happen in a few weeks. I didn't understand why he wasn't here today, and even more importantly, why did no one bring up the matter about the last phone call mum made to him, begging him to make the changes? I was incensed with Señor Ignacio but, for some reason it seemed like a waste of time. It all felt like it was a done deal anyway. I was annoyed he hadn't cross-examined Pedro. I wanted to shout out in the middle of the courtroom, "What are you doing? Ask him about the oxygen he was supposed to provide for my mum, to help her with her breathing, which never materialised!" I didn't dare, as I knew if I had said or done anything that may upset anyone, or the proceedings, the verdict could go in the opposite direction for me. Again, all I could do was go home and wait.

A few weeks later it was time for the final hearing, with the judge's ruling. I didn't attend. I didn't want to be anywhere near these people and Señor Ignacio thought it would be a waste of time; and as soon as they had finished, he would call me at home. It was the call I had been awaiting for over sixteen months. "*Hola*, Evie, how are you?"

"Well, just sitting here waiting to hear from you."

"I have good news for you. The judge has awarded you, '*La Legitima*'." I broke down and starting crying. Thank God, at least it was better than nothing. I had been so angry on behalf of mum. Had she known this was going to happen she would have done things so differently. If she were looking down and watching all that was going on, I know she would have been absolutely fuming. I wasn't really bothered about "*La Legitima*", I was more concerned about mum's final wishes being carried out and the stress she went through during the last forty-eight hours she was alive. I was happy Pedro wasn't going to be able to claim everything, even with the far-fetched stories to keep me from even the smallest amount of inheritance. I was relieved it was finally all over and we could get on with our lives.

Liam and I flew over a couple of weeks later to sign more paperwork and receive the bank cheque from the courts for the amount due. It wasn't the correct amount, but again it didn't matter. Justice had been done. I was thankful to the judge; she knew what was going on, I could see it in her face. She sympathised with me, but she didn't have the evidence, concrete evidence to prove anything, for or against, especially with my absent witnesses. The entire court hearing was recorded onto a CD, both the session I attended and the one I didn't. To this day it sits in a drawer in my desk, I am still unable to listen to it. I know it's full of lies but there is nothing I can do about it. Did Pedro pay a visit to the *gestor*? Did he tell him not to do anything, not to process anything? How could the *gestor* forget having a conversation with my mum?

The two solicitors are working together all the time. They probably see each other every day in different court hearings dealing with different cases. Friendly handshakes, a drink in the bar afterwards, they still had to work together. Was there a... "Let's make this as easy as possible. Don't push too hard on this. Don't ask too many questions about certain topics." This may well have been the case. God is a higher Judge, and He would take care of it. All I could do was to let it go.

Finally, back in England, there was peace and some sort of closure. I find it hard, sometimes, to think Pedro has most of her money, her apartments, her jewellery collection. It's the little things I miss most, like the various smells from her collection of perfumes - insignificant to him but hugely significant to me. I couldn't help thinking how his children would be enjoying all the things my children should. I wasn't bothered for myself, but I was annoyed for mum's grandchildren. For so many years I worked with her, helped her with so many things, and I was never paid any wages. She didn't have to pay me, but it was the fact of how she always said, "Evie, all this is going to be yours one day, don't you worry. When I die all of this is going to be yours: I have nobody else to give it to. You are my flesh and blood." How wrong she was. How ironic!

There was sadness in my heart but an inexplicable peace as well. A quiet inner reassurance filled me, I was at rest. Everything was fine and everything was going to continue to be fine. I had a small inner voice saying, "Everything you've lost will be regained, but not as you know it."

Finally, I could begin to grieve for both my mum and my dad. It is true what they say, "Life does go on," and I have been so blessed to have Liam's love and support throughout, and my two boys who bring me so much joy.

A few months later, I was pregnant with our third child. Our little princess, Sophie, was born - my little gift from Heaven. I remember when mum died and I sat with her in the *tanatorio,* when the time had come to say my final goodbye as they removed her from the glass unit, I placed three red roses in her hand. "Mum, I have three beautiful red roses for you. One is from your grandson Oscar, one is from your other grandson James, and this one, Mum, is from me." Tears streamed down my face as they took her away for the final time. I look back and think about those three roses I gave her, they were from Oscar, James, and Sophie, who was yet to arrive.

So much has happened since that moment when I sat beside my mum in the hospital room, with the sun streaming through the window as I held her hand and sang songs to her. I wish things had been different, but at least we got to make amends and we found peace together. At least she knew I loved her, and she had confessed so much to me, repenting, asking for forgiveness. Those last forty-eight hours were so precious, no one can take them away from me, not even Pedro.

God had answered what would seem to be the most complicated biggest prayer. Even though mum and I lived in separate countries, I was with her, right by her side, her in my arms and dying without any fear. God had answered all those prayers. He was with me the whole time.

Life returned to normal, whatever normal looks like. Liam settled back into running the bar, restaurant and nightclub and I was busy bringing up our three beautiful children. We felt blessed and we were thankful. Life was good but I wondered if this was it. This couldn't be it surely? Something inside me said it wasn't, that little inner voice told me it wasn't and there was so much more to come. But I didn't know what.

**"With the redemptive power of God,
the worst events become the brightest future."**

Neil Thompson

Director of ESST
Edinburgh School of Supernatural Transformation

BOOK TWO

VICTORIOUS SPIRIT

Chapter 1

Pézenas, France, February 2005

The thief comes only to steal and kill and destroy;
I have come that they may have life, and have it to the full.
-John 10:10 NIV

This was the second house we had viewed, and I was starting to lose my patience with the estate agent. "I asked for four bedrooms, a property that has four bedrooms! Why are you showing me a property with only three? And this garden is tiny. We're really looking for a garden with space for the children."

Why we had to be accompanied by three agents I had no idea. I just wanted to deal with one person. There was no need for the whole entourage.

"Okay. Okay, Madam, I will take you. I have something better for you. You do not like this one? I have another one for you. Let's go. We'll go in the car." I was fed up by this point. I knew what I wanted. I had given them a description of what we were looking for property wise. Why could they not just show us a property that met our requirements?

We pulled up outside another townhouse in the middle of a housing estate with a tiny front garden. I knew this wasn't the one either, but the two French men and woman showing us round seemed to have their own agenda by showing us exactly the opposite of what we were looking for. We went into the house, it was dark and dingy, in need of redecorating and a whole new kitchen. The bathroom needed plumbing. It looked like someone had started renovating the place but not managed to finish it. "This won't do at all! I need a bathroom, a fully fitted bathroom, not one with a separate toilet. We like to have the toilet in the bathroom. This is nothing like what I have asked to see. You are just wasting our time. I told you we do not want this type of property. I told you we didn't like this area. Why do you keep showing me what I haven't asked for? There are only two bedrooms, there are five of us!" It was not going well.

Earlier that morning, when we were in the office, we specifically told Natalie the estate agent, what we were looking for, but she didn't give us any options, she just told us to get in the car and they would show us some of the properties they had on their books. Usually, one would look at the options first to see if they were of any interest and then decide if it was worth visiting them or not. We were running out of time; we were heading back to England the next day and my window of opportunity to buy our dream house would be closed for another few months or even a year. I really thought we were going to find something this time, especially as Liam had finally come around to the idea. I didn't want him to change his mind.

I knew something was waiting for us somewhere. It wasn't as if we were looking for something out of the ordinary, just something nice with a half decent garden. It didn't need to be huge or have lots of land, just big enough for the kids to play in and for Sydney, our beautiful German Shepherd dog - but we did want four bedrooms so each of our children could have their own room. If there were a spare one then that would be a bonus for when family and friends came to visit, and maybe an office. An office would be nice, something a little special.

There was nothing wrong in wanting something a little bit special.

But now, we had run out of time. Uncle Ian and Aunty Carol were waiting for us back at their house. We were all going out for lunch before getting ready for our drive back home to England. That was it. I felt as if my dream was slowly, slipping through my fingers, out of reach. We said goodbye to the estate agents Pierre and Antoine, but Natalie stayed behind and waited with us by the car. We dealt with her initially. She was friendly and seemed a nice lady. "You didn't like any of these properties, did you?"

"No, they weren't what we're looking for." She could see the frustration on my face.

"I have a house to show you. I think this is it. It is just what you are looking for. It is slightly out of your budget and does need some work, but it is ideal for you. I know you will love this house; I know this is what you're looking for." At this point, Liam had had enough.

"No, that's fine. We are not looking at any more houses. We are staying at home this afternoon and we're travelling back tomorrow. We are not interested. That's it." Liam had spoken.

Natalie looked me straight in the eye. "You're going to love this property. This property is for you. I know it. As long as you don't mind doing a bit of work."

"Well, we don't mind doing a bit of work if it's for the right property. We want to live in it, so we will have plenty of time. We could do it up slowly. But we go back tomorrow. Can't we see it this afternoon?"

Liam spoke again and was adamant. "No, we're not seeing any more properties. That is it. I have had enough. Let's go."

Natalie was insistent. "I can arrange a viewing for you for tomorrow morning. What time are you leaving?"

"We're leaving at about half-past nine, maybe ten." I looked at

Liam with his head in his hands, shaking his head.

"I could probably get a viewing arranged for you for ten o'clock in the morning. Let me speak to the owners and you can view it on your way back."

Liam, at this point was huffing. "Really? We are not doing this. We're not going to view any more properties!"

"Oh, please, Honey, please. You never know, this might be the one. What if this is the one and we miss it? She says it's got everything we want and more."

"It has five bedrooms and a nice big garden. I'm telling you, you will love it," Natalie interjected.

"Yes, that sounds good. Is it in a village? I don't want to be out in the sticks in the middle of nowhere."

"It's just as you come into the village. You can walk into the centre, no problem."

"Oh, Honey, please. Can we? This could be it. Let's not miss it."

"Okay then, alright, but it will have to be first thing in the morning. If the owners can't do it, then that is it. We need to hit the road; we've got a long drive ahead of us." I grabbed him by the neck and gave him a big kiss on the cheek.

"Okay, good, let me call the owners and I'll let you know later on," said Natalie.

"Thank you, Honey. Thank you." I gave Liam another big hug and kiss. I was intrigued and very excited. Natalie took us back to the estate agent's office and handed us a printout with information about the house we were hoping to see. To my immense surprise it had a swimming pool and a huge garden, two thousand square metres of garden and one side of the house had a turret.

"Look at these photos," encouraged Natalie. "It does need a bit of TLC."

"That's fine. We can do that with time."

"I know it's over your budget, but they are willing to negotiate as it's been on the market for a while. They will accept an offer. Okay, see you tomorrow."

I was so excited. I couldn't wait for tomorrow to come. We got back to Ian and Carol's; they had been having fun looking after the kids. We packed our bags, got everything ready for the next day and headed out to enjoy some lunch.

The next morning, we hugged Ian and Carol goodbye and we bundled into the car and headed towards the property. I had been reading and re-reading the information sheet about the house. It was in a nice sized village called Montagnac. It wasn't far from where Ian and Carol lived, a ten-minute drive away, and five minutes from the historic town of Pézenas, surrounded by vines and ten minutes from the port and beach of Mèze.

Liam was still not impressed. He had already given up. "We're not going to find what we're looking for. We can always come back another time, Evie. We don't have to get something now."

"Yes, but if this is the one then we'll have to act on it, we'll know when it's the right one."

We arranged to meet Natalie in the centre of the village. We pulled up at the top of the esplanade near the bakers just as we had been instructed. Along the esplanade, were a couple of bar-restaurants, their tables and chairs carefully positioned under the shade created by the tall, leafy plane trees, (the trees which shed their bark instead of their leaves) where people sat relaxing enjoying their morning coffee. There was a little supermarket, the choice of three bakers, a bank, and a pharmacy. The main square was in the centre of the historic part of the village where the French flag flew proudly over the *Marie*, the Mayor's office. Next to it stood a beautiful nine-hundred-year-old church. If you walked around the back streets of the village, you would stumble upon many medieval buildings and archways.

We remembered staying in this same village a couple of years ago when my cousin Daniel got married. We stayed just up the road in a boutique-type B&B. I was pregnant with our third child, Sophie, at the time. Today was market day and the village had a lovely vibe to it. From the top of the esplanade down towards the bars, local farmers and butchers had their stalls laid out with their colourful, fresh, seasonal produce. There was the local lady who sold rotisserie chicken with the added choice of roast potatoes or paella. The smell was amazing. Then you had the stalls selling shoes and clothes. It wasn't a huge market, but it had all the essentials you might need to see you through the week. You could see the locals bumping into each other, sharing the latest gossip. Everyone was so relaxed. Everything about it was perfect.

We greeted Natalie; she seemed excited. "Right. Are you ready? You are going to like this one. This is the one for you."

"Okay, stop building it up because it is out of our budget. We don't have much money. We will have to see how much work needs doing first." We got back into our cars and followed Natalie. We drove up the road towards the end of the village heading towards the sea. We drove past the village houses that lined the road, past the *Salle de Fete,* typically known as the village hall, and then past a little petrol station – that was handy – then Natalie turned left up into what seemed to be a small country road heading up into the vines. I hadn't noticed but behind some big trees and hedges, set up high up from the main road, hidden behind the trees, was the house we were going to see. We pulled up in front of a big black iron gate which opened onto a driveway.

"Right kids, this is it. We're going to have to be very good and quiet as we look at this house," I warned the children.

"Wow, Mummy, this house is so big!" exclaimed Oscar excitedly.

"It is lovely, isn't it? I agreed. "Now, don't forget we are just going to have a look at it, that's all," I reminded everyone while looking at Liam, with a reassuring look so he knew I hadn't moved into the house just yet.

We parked and walked up the small driveway where there was another set of gates, green this time. A beautiful large house stood before us with its large front garden. The house sat in the middle of two thousand square metres of land. As we walked up the wide garden path, I observed a great veranda that wrapped itself around the front of the house and continued around the side. We walked in through the veranda and rang the doorbell to the front door. I could see us sitting out here drinking coffee, the kids playing, doing some painting.

"Mummy, look, it has a conservatory. It's bigger than ours." James was itching to go and explore.

"Don't forget, we have to be good."

The front door opened, and we were greeted by the owner who seemed to be in her early seventies, she had one of her sons with her. They were pleased to see us. Natalie was permitted to show us around the house herself while the owners went and sat in the front garden and waited. We started with the kitchen which was immediately to our left, the dark brown cabinets and brown tiles on the walls needed updating, there was a glass door which led out onto the veranda where you could have your lunch. The veranda was so lovely and bright. We then proceeded into the living room. There, lit and roaring, was a large fire, beautiful stone surround and wooden beams on the ceiling. One of the nice things about the inviting living room was how it led around into the dining room. At the far end of the dining room was a sweeping marble staircase that went up into the turret, the circular part of the house.

The floor tiles were nice enough, a creamy, mottled beige. We climbed the marble stairs which seemed to grow out of the wall, to where we were surprised to find another lounge and two bedrooms, and a room which was crying out to be converted into a lovely shower room. It was an entire apartment in itself. While we were there, Natalie showed us the loft space. We opened the door, and the loft ran along the whole length of the house. We could convert this space and create even more rooms if needed. We went back downstairs, opened the dining room doors and walked out into the garden. Right in front of us was a swimming pool and a lovely, covered terrace area. Already, I could see us having lunch, dinners and parties with people swimming and jumping into the pool, our very own pool. We hadn't asked for a pool, so this was amazing. We walked around the garden, all two thousand square metres of it. There was a pool house where all the cleaning materials for maintaining the pool lived. There was even a robot for cleaning the pool. Liam loved that idea. There were olive trees and some fruit trees; it was an orchard.

None of the property was overlooked; it was incredibly secluded and private. Back in the house, we walked through the lounge back towards the front door and turned left down a long hallway. Off the hallway were three more bedrooms, a toilet, a separate family bathroom and through one of the bedrooms a very large office space with patio doors looking out to the front garden. The bedroom also led into a laundry room, the biggest laundry room I have ever seen, with shelving space for storing all your towels and bed linen and more. The master bedroom was enormous. This one was going to be mine. At one end of the room was a giant mirror. It was as if it had been a dance studio. Every bedroom on this ground floor had a door that led out onto the terrace and the swimming pool. The kids ran excitedly around the house, choosing bedrooms. Liam looked at me. He knew what I was thinking. There is so much work to be done here. The wallpaper in the lounge and dining room was from the 1970s. It was quite nice, not bad, green. It wasn't garish, you could live with it, but it did need updating. The potential in this house was incredible, and the size was impressive. It was nearly three times the size of our house in England, and it ticked all our boxes and more. It was our dream house.

There was an office, five good-sized bedrooms, two lounge areas and a dining room. At the end of the drive was a secret path that led up to the vines, miles and miles of vines which would be ideal for walking our dog, Sydney. We had fallen in love with this house; we absolutely loved it. The swimming pool had its winter cover on. It was a big pool, ten by five metres with Roman steps. The owners lifted a corner of the heavy faded blue protective covering, and I could see the Roman steps going into the pool. It looked incredible. "Is everything alright with the pool? There are no problems?" I asked.

"Oh, yes, it works. There's nothing wrong with it at all."

"Okay, that's good." I felt reassured, there was no need to ask for the very well secured winter cover to be removed, for me to inspect it myself.

I glanced around the outside of the house. The house was a faded salmon colour, not even salmon pink, but a faded cream colour that would need repainting. There was a garage big enough for two or three cars. Liam liked the look of the garage, I could see his face when we walked in, his eyes lit up and his mouth turned upwards into a smile. And there was even more. There was an area at the back of the house which would be ideal for growing vegetables. Again, Liam's eyes started to sparkle. Now I had his attention.

"What do you do with the olives? Do you harvest them?" I asked the owner.

"You can process them yourself, or you can take them to the local olive cooperative."

"Okay." We could not believe what we were seeing. The children were running around the garden; they were in their element. We all kept an eye on where they were because of the swimming pool. That year the French government had passed a new law where every swimming pool had to either have an alarm system or be fully enclosed. That was yet to be installed in this property.

We said our goodbyes, shook hands with Natalie, got in our cars and drove off.

I had to wait, bide my time. I knew how to approach Liam without overwhelming him. I had to go slowly and gently when it came to sharing my view and thoughts with him - especially if I needed him to agree with me. I wanted this house; this house was going to be ours. The children loved it. They had already chosen their bedrooms and I had chosen ours. As they were running around, they had spotted two trees perfect for climbing. They looked so carefree and happy.

Liam and I started to discuss the pros and cons. "Honey, it's got five bedrooms. One of those bedrooms is massive, we can convert it and have six bedrooms. One for your mum and dad and one for our friends, and that office is great! The room upstairs, that can be the children's playroom. They would have a playroom - and that swimming pool...! We could never have imagined having that sort of property."

Before joining the motorway and heading north, we decided to see what was at the end of the road, see where it led.

Having driven through the beautiful countryside and vines as far as the eye could see, we arrived in a town called Mèze. Again, we sat in our car, bemused. This must be a dream. We had discovered the beautiful, quaint, coastal village of Mèze right on the Étang de Thau. In years gone by it used to be popular for its fishing, now it was famous for its oyster farming and the selection of seafood restaurants that adorned the port. We had a quick drive around the harbour and just around the corner was a beach. It was such a pretty town. It didn't get better than this.

"Mummy, look at the boats!" The children were staring out of the car windows, excited to see all the different coloured fishing boats and small yachts.

"I know, isn't it exciting? And look at the lovely little beach and the restaurant. Next time we're in the area, we will come back and have lunch here."

"Yeah!" shouted Sophie.

Unfortunately, time was pressing on and we didn't have time to hang around. I didn't want to leave, I had already moved in. The thought of having all this at the end of the road filled my heart with joy. We followed the signs back towards the motorway. I waited as long as I could.

"So, what are your thoughts, Honey?"

"I think it's brilliant. It's close to Ian and Carol's, and it's right where we want to be. It's everything we've ever wanted and more."

"Can we afford it though?" I asked as I held my breath, dreading the reply.

"Well, if we sold our house and cut back on our spending, we could just about afford it, but we would have to get a small mortgage."

"Would we be able to get a mortgage?"

"I don't know. Let me make some phone calls." I held my breath.

"Do you have a pen and paper in your handbag?" I promptly had them at the ready while Liam dictated some numbers to me, and I noted down all the calculations.

"How much do you think we could get for our house? How much mortgage do you think we'd need?" I asked impatiently.

"Will you just wait and let me figure it out. Let's talk about this calmly." My questions were bombarding poor Liam. We had a long drive ahead with nothing better to talk about.

The children were now happily settled in the back, having finally decided what film to watch first.

"Oh, not *Barbie* again!" moaned poor Oscar.

"Honey, I don't want us to lose this house. If somebody else sees this house and puts an offer in, we could lose it." Liam knew he had already lost. As we drove over the snow-covered Massif Central mountains, Liam made some phone calls to our financial adviser to see if we could get a mortgage - and how much we could get.

"So, Paul, how much would the repayments be?" Liam listened attentively to Paul on the other end of the phone, while I sat next to him praying it would all work out. "And what if I sold those other shares?" So many questions were being asked over the phone as we drove through France. I sat beside him quietly, with pen and paper making notes as directed by Liam's finger-pointing, or head nodding.

After a couple of hours of phone calls to and from England, Liam had made the decision: "Yes, we can afford it."

"Really? Are you sure?" I didn't want to get too excited. I wanted to be sure I had heard right.

"Yes, we can."

"So, what do we do now?"

"Let's make them an offer."

"Oh, my goodness! Really? Really, Honey? Oh my gosh! I love you. I love you so much, Honey. How much should we offer them?"

"We'll offer them 20,000 euros under what they're asking because there's so much work to do."

"Okay, but what if they say no?"

"Well, let's start with that. Let's see what the owners say." I picked up the phone and called Natalie. I was shaking. "Natalie? It's Evie. How are you?"

"I'm good thanks. How are you?"

"We're driving through the mountains. We've been talking and made some phone calls. We'd like to make an offer on the house."

"Really? Oh, my word, that is so exciting."

"I know, I know. We would like to offer 20,000 euros under the asking price as it's over our budget and there's a lot of work to be done. But we love the house. Please see what you can do for us."

"Okay, I will. I'll call you back shortly." I put the phone down and we waited. I could hardly breathe. Ten minutes later the phone rang. I was so nervous. Please say yes, please say yes. "Evie?"

"Yes, I am here, but I may lose reception very soon. Did you manage to get hold of the owners?"

"Yes, and they've accepted."

"They've accepted?" I couldn't believe what I was hearing.

"Yes. They are more than happy to go ahead. Congratulations!"

"Oh, my word! Thank you so much. Thank you! I'm so happy!" Happy was not the word, I was beside myself. This was amazing. I put the phone down. "Liam, they've accepted our offer." The children's faces beamed with joy. "Liam, we've just bought a house."

Liam was trying to concentrate on his driving but was just as happy as I was.

"How did we do that? We visited a house today in France, are heading back to England, and we've just bought a house while driving over snow-covered mountains. That is crazy. How did that happen?" I said astounded.

"I don't know, Babe, but we just bought a house! We're moving to France!"

...to be continued.

AFTERWORD

So much has happened in the last eighteen years since the final chapter of Unvanquished Spirit. From exciting new beginnings in the South of France to walking through hell in Australia and suffering from PTSD and anxiety. And yet, with every new chapter comes a new awakening, a growing of trust, a deepening of my relationship with God and hearing His unmistakable voice. All this is recounted in my next book; Victorious Spirit.

My future is brighter and better than ever, but even though life may send challenges my way, they are now met with total reassurance knowing God is in control - but only if I choose to let Him. From the moment I recognised how He has brought me through everything, I knew He would continue to guide me in the future. Life would be so much better if I decided to acknowledge Him and chose to interact with Him. The only way to express my gratitude for everything He has done for me, and for never leaving my side, is to surrender my life to Him and serve Him. The moment I did this and followed it through was the moment I felt freedom and the peace of never having to worry about anything again.

The whole purpose of 'Unvanquished Spirit' and 'Victorious Spirit' is and always has been, to inspire and encourage you. I only hope that you will arrive at the same point I have, through all that happens in your life. I pray that you have the same incredible relationship with Him as well, and if you don't know Him yet, you will begin to seek Him as soon as possible.

Do you know Him?

If you would like to know the hope, love, healing, and peace that He brings, along with the forgiveness of all your sins, through His son Jesus Christ, who died on the cross for you; all you have to do is ask Him into your life, acknowledge the wrongs you have done and turn from them, He will lead you on the path you were meant to walk on. You can start with this simple yet extremely powerful prayer:-

Dear Lord Jesus,
Thank you for dying on the cross for my sin. Please forgive me.
Come into my life. I receive You as my Lord and Saviour. Now,
help me to live for you the rest of this life.
In the name of Jesus, I pray.
Amen

This short prayer of salvation is taken from
https://www.learnreligions.com/a-prayer-of-salvation-701284

If you have questions about prayer or want more information, why not visit some of your local churches or consider one of the following:
Alpha.org is a great course to do if you have questions about life. You can ask them at Alpha. Alpha is a place to ask the big questions of life. Connect with others online to watch a series of episodes and explore the Christian faith together.
https://www.alpha.org

Trypraying.com If you've never prayed before, why don't you try praying? It's easier than you think. Trypraying is a simple 7 day prayer guide for those who are not religious. You can get the booklet or download the app from their website.
https://www.trypraying.com

The Lord's Prayer

Our Father in heaven,
hallowed be your name,
your kingdom come,
your will be done,
on earth as in heaven.
Give us today our daily bread.
Forgive us our sins
as we forgive those who sin against us.
Lead us not into temptation
but deliver us from evil.
For the kingdom, the power,
and the glory are yours
now and forever.
Amen.
Church of England Version from Matthew 6:9-13

The Grace

May the grace of the Lord Jesus Christ,
and the love of God,
and the fellowship of the Holy Spirit be with you all,
evermore,
Amen
2 Corinthians 13:14– New International Version (NIV)

Bibles Verses

I sought the Lord, and he answered me; he delivered me from all my fears. - Psalm 34:4 NIV

The light shines in the darkness, and the darkness has not overcome it. - John 1:5 NIV

The Lord himself goes before you and will be with you; he will never leave you nor forsake you. -Deuteronomy 31:8 NIV

Start children off on the way they should go, and even when they are old they will not turn from it. -Proverbs 22:6 NIV

May your father and your mother be glad and let her rejoice who gave birth to you. -Proverbs 23:25 NIV

Children's children are a crown to the aged, and parents are the pride of their children -Proverbs 17:6 NIV

Then you will call on me and come and pray to me, and I will listen to you. - Jeremiah 29:12 NIV

For our light and momentary troubles are achieving for us an eternal glory that far outweighs them all. - 2 Corinthians 4:17 NIV

The body, however, is not meant for sexual immorality but for the Lord, and the Lord for the body. - 1 Corinthians 6:13 NIV

"Have I not commanded you? Be strong and courageous. Do not be afraid; do not be discouraged, for the Lord your God will be with you wherever you go." - Joshua 1:9 NIV

Pray continually. - 1 Thessalonians 5:17 NIV

For this reason a man will leave his father and mother and be united to his wife, and the two will become one flesh. -Ephesians 5:31 NIV

Listen to my words: "When there is a prophet among you, I, the LORD, reveal myself to them in visions, I speak to them in dreams." -Numbers 12:6 NIV

Blessed are the meek, for they will inherit the earth. -Matthew 5:5 NIV

"Lord, how many times shall I forgive my brother or sister who sins against me? Up to seven times?" Jesus answered, "I tell you, not seven times, but seventy-seven times." -Matthew 18:21-23 NIV

They will have no fear of bad news; their hearts are steadfast, trusting in the LORD. -Psalm 112:7 NIV

Blessed are those who mourn, for they will be comforted. -Matthew 5:4 NIV

Even though I walk through the darkest valley, I will fear no evil, for you are with me; your rod and your staff, they comfort me. -Psalm 23:4 NIV

For I know the plans I have for you," declares the LORD, "plans to prosper you and not to harm you, plans to give you hope and a future. -Jeremiah 29:11 NIV

The thief comes only to steal and kill and destroy; I have come that they may have life and have it to the full. -John 10:10 NIV

Printed in Great Britain
by Amazon

27391942R00152